Praise for *Inner and Outer*

"This outstanding handbook ref. realizations emerging from divine love and inner fulfillment."

—Deepak Chopra

"I greatly appreciate Sant Rajinder Singh Ji Maharaj's contribution here to the goal of peace that we are all working towards. May readers of this book find peace within themselves through meditation and so foster a greater sense of peace throughout the world."

—H.H. The Dalai Lama

"This outstanding meditation handbook is by a respected spiritual teacher. Singh's deep wisdom and sympathetic advice have brought spiritual benefit to thousands. Now he can help guide you on the path to divine love and fulfillment."

—*Personal Transformation Magazine*

"Rajinder Singh's book is food for the soul. It is an inspiring and informative source that speaks to both beginner and experienced travelers on the path of life. I was uplifted and rededicated myself to honoring my inner work."

—Steven Halpern, Recording Artist and educator

"Firmly rooted in traditional wisdom, the author faces contemporary questions and challenges squarely and in a non-sectarian way. *Inner and Outer Peace Through Meditation* goes to the essence of the matter. Its language is clear and forthright. It offers practical step-by-step exercises to bring the seed of peace within us to fruition in daily life and the world we live in."

—Brother David Steindl-Rast

*By the same author*

Inner and Outer Peace through Meditation
Ecology of the Soul
Education for a Peaceful World
Vision of Spiritual Unity and Peace

# Empowering Your Soul Through Meditation

Rajinder Singh

# ELEMENT

Boston, Massachusetts • Shaftesbury, Dorset
Melbourne, Victoria

© Element Books, Inc. 1999
Text © SK Publications 1999

First published in the USA in 1999 by
Element Books, Inc.
160 North Washington Street,
Boston, Massachusetts 02114

Published in Great Britain in 1999 by
Element Books Limited
Shaftesbury, Dorset SP7 8BP

Published in Australia in 1999 by
Element Books Limited for
Penguin Books Australia Limited
487 Maroondah Highway, Ringwood, Victoria 3134

**Library of Congress Cataloging-in-Publication data**
Rajinder Singh, 1943–
    Empowering your soul through meditation / Rajinder Singh. — 1st
ed.
        p.  cm.
    1. Meditation.  2. Soul.  I. Title.
BL627.R334    1999
291.4'35—dc21                                                      99-12800
                                                                        CIP

British Library Cataloguing in Publication data available

Printed and bound in the United States by Edwards Brothers

ISBN 1-86204-547-X

Dedicated to my spiritual teachers,

Sant Kirpal Singh Ji Maharaj
and Sant Darshan Singh Ji Maharaj,

who helped countless people
throughout the world empower their soul
through meditation

*Rajinder Singh*

7/27/99

# *Contents*

Acknowledgments    *viii*
Introduction    *ix*

**Part I**   *Qualities of the Empowered Soul*   *1*
   **Chapter 1** Qualities of the Empowered Soul   *3*
   **Chapter 2** Unlimited Wisdom   *9*
   **Chapter 3** Immortality   *21*
   **Chapter 4** Unconditional Love   *33*
   **Chapter 5** Fearlessness   *43*
   **Chapter 6** Connectedness   *53*
   **Chapter 7** Bliss   *65*

**Part II**   *Obstacles to Knowing Our Empowered Soul*   *77*
   **Chapter 8** Limited Vision   *79*
   **Chapter 9** Aimlessly Adrift   *87*
   **Chapter 10** Layers Covering the Soul   *95*

**Part III**   *How to Access the Unlimited Energy of Our Soul*   *117*
   **Chapter 11** Meditation: Doorway to the Soul   *119*
   **Chapter 12** Journey to Realms of Light Within Us   *133*
   **Chapter 13** Removing the Coverings of the Soul   *141*
   **Chapter 14** Finding Time for Our Self   *159*
   **Chapter 15** Looking Inward and Outward Simultaneously   *167*

Endnotes    *177*
About the Author    *179*

# *Acknowledgments*

I would like to acknowledge and thank my revered spiritual teachers, Sant Kirpal Singh Ji Maharaj (1894–1974) and Sant Darshan Singh Ji Maharaj (1921–1989), from whom I learned the practice of meditation. Sant Kirpal Singh Ji is known throughout the world today as the "Father of the Human Unity movement." Sant Darshan Singh Ji was recognized as one of the leading mystic poet-saints of modern times and received four Urdu Academy Awards for his poetry. in this book, I pass along to humanity the technique of empowering the soul that I learned from them.

I would like to express my gratitude for the love of my revered mother, Mata Harbhajan Kaur Ji, and the companionship of my dear wife, Rita Ji.

I would also like to thank Jay and Ricki Linksman for seeing the manuscript through to publication.

And I would like to thank God, the source of limitless love and countless blessings.

# Introduction

The most pressing need I find as I travel around the world is that people want to get in touch with their soul and their own spiritual dimensions. This book, *Empowering Your Soul through Meditation* has been written for all those who wish to explore the limitless potential of the soul. The book is designed to help readers explore the power and energy of the soul latent within each of us and use these to enrich and transform our lives. It is meant to awaken readers to the empowered soul and its rich qualities of unlimited wisdom, fearlessness, immortality, unconditional love, bliss, and connectedness to all life.

What are the blockages that keep us from tapping our inner gifts? How can we remove these blockages? Simple techniques are provided for accessing the riches of our soul so readers can discover for themselves their own potential. Once we tap these inner resources, we can experience a profound transformation that will enrich all areas of our life—from personal relations, to physical, mental, and emotional health, to our work, to our spiritual growth, and to the attainment of our life's goals. It is my hope that this transformation can bring peace and joy into our lives and can contribute to a more peaceful, loving world.

I humbly offer this book, *Empowering Your Soul Through Meditation*, in the hope that this simple handbook and guide will help readers explore the soul and realize its endless potential.

*Rajinder Singh*
*February 6, 1999*

# PART I    *Qualities of the Empowered Soul*

# Qualities of the Empowered Soul

Within us are riches greater than any we can ever accumulate on earth. We have inside us a source of knowledge from which all other knowledge flows. A love far greater and fulfilling than any we can know in the outer world is waiting to embrace us with open arms within. At our core is a strength and power that can enable us to overcome any fear. Underlying our separateness as individuals is a connectedness and oneness to all life. Awaiting us inside is a bliss and joy so fulfilling that we need no other intoxicants to make us happy. All these gifts lie within us in the empowered soul.

The soul is a source of tremendous wisdom, love, and power, yet we remain ignorant of its treasures when we allow it to be overpowered by the mind, the senses, and the physical body. When the mind and body assert power over the soul, the soul forgets itself. But the empowered soul is our true nature, and it is time we reclaim the soul so that its gifts can enrich our life.

There are two ways to view ourselves with regard to the soul. The first is to view ourselves primarily as a body and mind. When we see ourselves in this manner, we say that we are a mind and body that "have a soul." The second is to see ourselves primarily as a soul. When we change perspective and identify with the soul, we say that we are a soul who "has or wears a mind and body." To assess how we look at ourselves is one of our goals in *Empowering Your Soul Through Meditation*. If we think we are a mind and body, then ours is a journey to find the soul. If we realize that we are the soul, which has been given a mind and body to maneuver through the physical world, then our goal is to further empower the soul. By empowering the soul we recover its natural control over the mind and senses.

The aim of *Empowering Your Soul Through Meditation* is to help reacquaint us with the qualities of the soul and provide direction for its empowerment. The soul's power has been forgotten. The mind, the senses, the body, and the pulls of the physical world have placed the soul in a state of forgetfulness from which we must awaken. When we empower our soul, its wisdom, immortality, love, fearlessness, connectedness, and bliss add a new dimension to our life.

Many people live and die without ever realizing the full power and potential of their soul. At some time in their life, they may wonder about the soul, about God, and about the purpose of their existence. This search for meaning and purpose—the spiritual quest—is one that people pursue in individual ways. Some seek answers in scripture while others search in places of worship. Some go beyond their own religion to find the answers offered in other faiths. Whichever method one adopts, the direction one follows to find the answers to life's questions is known as the spiritual path. It is the spiritual path that leads to the realization of the inner self, to the soul.

Many people pass through life never realizing who they are and never certain about the purpose of their existence. In times of trouble or in the face of death, they may raise these questions, but may not follow them through to a fulfilling conclusion or else may abandon the process when the bad times pass. But those who have a burning desire to find the answers to the mysteries of life can find them.

Fortunately, there are people in the world who have found spiritual fulfillment and can guide us. If we look through history we find that in every generation there have been people who have realized themselves as soul and have realized God. Some of their wisdom and experiences have been recorded in history and, in some cases, a religion has been created from their teachings. Other realized souls have come and gone but have left behind no records because they did not found a religion or leave behind any scriptures. Some of them we know of through references by other people who wrote about them. One thing is clear: these realized souls have the ability to teach us how to realize ourselves. If we find such a being, we can learn how we, too, can discover our soul and its attributes. True knowledge comes from seeing and experiencing on our own. We may read what others write or listen to what others say, but we cannot be fully satisfied until we experience for ourselves.

This book touches on the two aspects of spiritual knowledge that can help us realize our soul: the theoretical knowledge, and the personal or practical knowledge. The theoretical side consists of what other realized people have said about the soul (such as what are some of its qualities—wisdom, immortality, fearlessness, love, connectedness, and bliss). The personal or practical side consists of a technique that I learned from a fully realized being. I wish to share this technique to help others realize their soul on their own.

On the theoretical side, a comparative study of religions reveals a basic agreement among them: that we are not just a physical body, but we are also the soul or spirit behind the body. It is the soul that gives us life. When the soul is in the body, we are physically alive. When the soul leaves the body at the time of death, the body ceases to exist. The body may perish, but the soul that inhabits it is immortal. The soul continues to exist after our physical death.

We are aware of our physical body because we can look at it, feel it, and listen to sounds coming from it. But where and what is the soul? How can we recognize it? What are its characteristics and qualities? This book provides a way for us to accomplish two tasks: the theoretical understanding of our true selves as soul, and the practical technique for the realization of our soul and the empowering of it to guide our lives.

From the outset, we should define certain terminology to ensure that there is no confusion in how words are being used throughout the book. The term "soul" is defined as our true essence or spiritual side—the part of us that lives beyond the death of our physical body. The soul exists whether it has a body or mind. When it enters this world, it is given a body and mind. As human beings, we are thus "embodied souls" or souls with a body and mind. The terms "we" and "us" refer to us as human beings or embodied souls. The process of finding the soul is referred to as "tapping into" or "discovering our soul within us." When we finally do discover our soul and identify with it as being our true nature, then the soul is referred to as the "empowered soul," a soul that has recognized itself and is aware that it is the essence of who we really are, that it is the guiding power behind the body and mind.

Some of us may spend our lives searching for knowledge in the outer world. Little do we know that the source of all answers, the universal wisdom, lies within us. That universal wisdom is another name for the state of being all-conscious. Some of us may find that at times our life is thwarted by fear and anxiety, hopelessness and depression; yet we have a source of fearlessness within us that can help us overcome inner turmoil. We fear death and the passing away of loved ones; but we do not realize that immortality is ours. We crave love and seek it in many places; but there is an unconditional love within that awaits us with open arms. We feel alone and disconnected in the world; but there is a place of unity and connectedness within us that, when accessed, can enhance our relationships with others, with nature, and with all life.

True joy is not as elusive as we think. We can find lasting happiness if we only look in the right place. Within us lies the unlimited power and energy of the empowered soul. Its rich qualities include wisdom, fearlessness, immortality, unconditional love, connectedness, and bliss. Tapping into the soul and its powers can enrich and transform our life.

We remain ignorant of these inner gifts because blockages keep us from tapping into them. How can we remove these blockages? What process do we need to employ to discover all that we seek?

There are simple techniques for accessing the riches of our soul. We need not search the four corners of the earth. We need not travel into outer space. These techniques can be practiced in the comfort of our home.

Once we learn to tap into our inner resources, we can experience a profound transformation that can enrich all areas of our life—personal relations; physical, mental, and emotional health; professional work; spiritual growth; and the attainment of our life's goals. This transformation cannot only bring peace and joy to our lives, but can also contribute to a peaceful, loving world.

The aim of this book is to provide a means by which we can re-identify with the soul (i.e., realize that the mind and body are merely our soul's outer coverings through which it can live and work in this physical world) and to empower the soul to guide our life.

# *Unlimited Wisdom* 2

What is the empowered soul? What is the source of its unlimited wisdom? The soul is all-knowing because it is a part of God. Anyone who has a belief in God assumes that God knows everything. Parents tell children, "Beware. God is watching your every thought, word, and deed." In the Old Testament, Adam and Eve, who were forbidden by God to eat fruit from the Tree of Knowledge, disobeyed Him. They tried to hide their disobedience, but they discovered there was nowhere to hide from God, the all-knowing being. God expelled them from the Garden of Eden, and we, their children, have been trying to find the gate back to the garden ever since.

Our search to find the garden can be seen in our exploration to find answers to the nature of our physical universe. For example, in a large lab in Batavia, Illinois, scientists accelerate atomic particles at high speed through a giant ring deep inside the earth, only to smash them to bits. They are searching for the "God particle"—their name for the particle that will give them answers to how our universe began. Along the way, they have discovered numerous subatomic particles with exotic names such as bosons, quarks, mesons, etc. While they have learned much about the nature of matter and energy, they have not yet found the ultimate answer they are seeking.

Other scientists measure the distance of the farthest quasars in the universe to calculate how long ago the theorized "Big Bang" took place in which they believe the whole universe emerged from the ignition of dust particles. They believe that they know much about what transpired in the first few milliseconds after the Big Bang, but aggressively seek to find out what existed before the Big Bang. From where did the first particles come? Science has so far failed to answer this question, but the race to be the first to solve the mystery continues.

In medical research labs throughout the world, scientists are working to unravel the genetic code of human DNA. With the help of computers, every part of our genetic make-up is being analyzed and coded to categorize the portions of our DNA that determine every aspect of our life, from our physical body and brain to how our body contracts and fights certain diseases. Does our genetic code hold the mystery to who we are as human beings?

Are we alone in our search for the answers to life and the universe? They wonder if we are the only life forms in creation. Some scientists beam impulses far into deep space in the hope that one day a response will come back from a distant galaxy. How big is space? Is it truly infinite, or do the ends of space meet, making the galaxy one, large sphere? If it is a sphere, what lies beyond it? These questions tempt humanity to undertake dangerous and expensive voyages into space in the hope that someday we can venture far enough to find out about the nature of our universe.

In computer labs, engineers experiment with artificial intelligence. Will they succeed to build a computer that thinks like a human being? Are human beings merely like complex computer programs whose function can be replicated by robots, or are they unique beings, inhabited by a nonmaterial soul, that defy man-made replication?

Some physicists are using the mathematical formulae of physics to prove the existence of God and the soul on paper. According to some of their interpretation of the statistics of the universe, there *is* a supreme power that both created the universe and sustains it, and that will draw the universe back unto itself in the distant future.

Geologists and paleontologists in remote parts of the world excavate the earth, searching for fossils and rocks to understand the nature of early human beings and other forms of life. Each new discovery pushes the date of the earliest life forms back. Scientists hope to either prove or disprove earlier scientific theories of evolution, but how such marvelous creatures came to be still eludes both sides.

In emergency rooms throughout the world, doctors listen intently to the experiences of patients who were revived from clinical death. These near-death experiences challenge the scientific world by their frequency of occurrence and striking similarities. They add anecdotal evidence to the theory of existence beyond the physical realm and shatter the egocentric thinking of humans that the earth and this universe are alone in creation.

The researchers and methodologies may differ, but at the heart of all of this searching lies the same burning questions: What is this world about? How did it come into being? Does God exist? Do we have a soul? Where did the soul come from and where does it go when physical life ends? Is there a purpose to our life?

Scientists, researchers, engineers, and doctors spend their whole life researching pieces of the puzzle. The mystery is so vast that no one person can study all its aspects, but each must specialize in one small area. Some explore the puzzle through biology, others through astronomy or geology or physics. But the physical sciences have their limitations. A lifetime of seeking the answers to our place in the universe through science has not, so far, yielded conclusive results. The reason that this outer search has not succeeded is that the answers to life's mysteries lie not outside, but within each of us. The mystery of the macrocosm is contained in the microcosm.

Science tells us that the universe is composed of matter and energy. But how do matter and energy explain consciousness? We know there is a difference between a living person and one who has died, but the matter that makes up both is the same. The body that has died is composed from the same material that composes the body when it was alive. But the part of that human being who communicated to us, that created, that controlled movement of the body, has departed. The being's consciousness has departed.

We recognize that human beings are conscious beings. A person whose heart and breathing have stopped is said to have "lost physical consciousness." But where does the consciousness encased in matter originate? If our soul is the conscious part of us, then there must be a source from where the soul originates. Is it created out of the matter and energy of the universe? We know that there is no consciousness in matter. We know there is no consciousness in physical energy.

Many modern scientists no longer believe that they have to be atheists to keep their scientific "faith." In fact, the more the scientists discover about scientific laws, the more they acknowledge the possibility of the existence of a higher intelligent power that designed creation. The miracle of the human body, the wonder of the earth, and the awesome universe with its seemingly countless galaxies all seem to be more than a chance accident of nature. Indeed, the mysterious atom, the complex genetic code, and the creation of this entire universe seem more a proof of God's existence.

While science grapples with questions about God and the soul, another segment of humanity has been doing research using different methodology. Known as prophets, saints, mystics, enlightened beings, and spiritual masters, these enlightened ones have had a profound impact on humanity throughout the ages. Their discoveries have touched a chord in the human heart, causing millions of people to proclaim themselves disciples or believers. World religions have grown out of the teachings of these enlightened individuals. Why are their messages so powerful that they can inspire the lives of people centuries after they have departed the physical world?

The answer lies in the fact that they discovered answers to the questions that every human being faces at one time or another in his or her life. They discovered the unlimited wisdom of the empowered soul.

## What Have Enlightened Ones Discovered About the Soul and God?

What the saints and prophets discovered is that God and the soul are one and the same. They found that the soul is of the same essence as God. It is but a particle or drop of the entire ocean that is God. Every major religion recognizes the oneness of God and the soul.

In the Bible, it is written:

> God said, "Let us make human beings in our image, after our likeness."
>
> (Genesis 1.26)

In Buddhism, while the term God is not used, there is recognition of the Buddha nature:

> Every being has the Buddha nature. This is the self.
>
> (Mahaparinirvana Sutra 214)

In the Qur'an, it is written:

> I have breathed into man of My spirit.
>
> (Qur'an 15:29)

In the teachings of Hinduism, it is said:

> In the golden city of the heart dwells
> The Lord of Love, without parts, without stain.

> *Know him as the radiant light of lights.*
> *There shines not the sun, neither moon nor star,*
> *Nor flash of lightning, nor fire lit on earth.*
> *The Lord is the light reflected by all,*
> *He shining, everything shines after him.*
>
> (Mundaka Upanishad 2.2.10-11)

And again:

> *At whose behest does the mind think?*
> *Who bids the body live?*
> *Who makes the tongue speak?*
> *Who is that effulgent Being that directs the eye to form and*
>     *color and the ear to sound?*
> *The Self (Atman) is ear of the ear, mind of the mind, speech of*
>     *speech.*
> *He is also breath of the breath, and eye of the eye.*
> *Having given up the false identification of the Self with the*
>     *senses and the mind, and knowing the Self to be Brahman,*
>     *the wise, on departing this life, become immortal.*
>
> (Kena Upanishad 1.1-2)

It is written in the Sikh holy book:

> *Our soul is the image of the Transcendent God.*
>
> (Sri Guru Granth Sahib, Gond, M.5, p. 868)

 ## Outer Theoretical Knowledge Can Only Point the Way to Unlimited Wisdom

Historical references provide us with outer, theoretical knowledge that can point out the direction we should search to find the soul, but does not help us become an empowered soul. We may look at what these references have to say, but without doing our own inner work we will not know for ourselves the validity of their statements. Theoretical knowledge is limited in its capacity to teach, as opposed to practical knowledge, which is gained from firsthand experience.

The Hindus have said in the Bhagavad Gita:

> *This is true knowledge: to seek the Self as the true end of wisdom always. To seek anything else is ignorance.*
>
> (Bhagavad Gita 13.11)

In Taoism, one finds:

> *True wisdom is different from much learning;*
> *Much learning means little wisdom.*
>
> (Tao Te Ching 81)

Knowing that there have been other people who have found their soul and God cannot give us self-realization. Knowing that the goal is attainable, however, is nonetheless inspiring. What others have done, we can also do. Knowing that a human being has walked on the moon drives scientists to build better spacecraft to fly even farther so that a human being can one day walk on distant planets. In the same manner, previous explorers of the inner voyage can inspire, motivate, and encourage us to follow in their path.

Knowing what saints and mystics have said about the empowered soul and its unlimited wisdom may move us to take steps to experience this ocean of knowledge. The scriptures and teachings of past saints are roadmaps or blueprints to reach our true potential.

The Buddhist parable of the raft gives us insight into the difference between scriptural knowledge and inner wisdom. A man on a journey comes to the shore of a sea. There is danger on the shore he has reached, but he learns that the opposite shore is safe. He wishes to go to the other side of the sea, but there is neither bridge to cross nor boat to carry him, so he decides to build his own vessel. He collects wood and leaves and constructs a small raft. Using his arms and legs to propel it, he successfully uses the raft to reach the other shore.

On the other side the man thinks, "This raft has helped me so far. I shall continue to carry it on my head and back as I cross the land, for it has helped me before." Thus, the man hauls the raft on his back like a donkey, although it is now a burden and is no longer useful to him.

In examining the actions of the man, the Buddhist parable leads us to conclude that it would be better if the man left the raft on the beach and went his way on foot. The raft is for crossing over water, not for carrying on one's head.

Many of us are like the man in this parable; the outer theoretical teachings and scriptures of world religions are like the raft. While the latter can help us go in the right direction, these outer words cannot help us on the other shore of the inner worlds. From that point on, we need direct experience. The teachings can lead us in the right direction, but they can't carry us to the truth.

## Where Are the Empowered Soul and God?

There is another story, told in many variations, but whose message is always the same. The story tells how God, wanting to go into seclusion but pretending not to know where to hide, consulted some wise advisors to test their wits.

"Why don't you hide Yourself on top of a mountain?" suggested one advisor.

"That won't work," sighed God. "People will eventually climb the mountain and discover Me."

"How about deep under the sea?" mentioned another savant.

"In time, people will learn how to dive and will find Me," said God.

"How about far out in space?" offered a third.

"One day, human beings shall penetrate space and locate Me," God replied.

At last, an advisor had the perfect solution. "I know a place where no one will ever look," he said.

"Where is that?" asked the others.

"Hide yourself in the human heart. No one will ever think to look there!" And God, taking this advice, did so, and has been hidden there ever since.

## Can Inner Wisdom Help Us Understand Our Purpose in Life?

For some, the questions of the universe, of creation and of life and death, are too remote from their everyday life. They are too entrenched in grappling with the day-to-day issues—What job should I pursue? Who should I marry? Where should I send my children to college? Questions that face us at our life's end do not seem relevant to the here and now. Can the unlimited wisdom of our empowered soul help us face life's daily questions and find our purpose in life as well?

Let us first define "unlimited wisdom." It is not the intellectual knowledge that we learn from lectures or books; it is consciousness. God is described as being "consciousness." Our soul, being the same essence as God, is also consciousness. It is a "state of knowing all that is to be known." When we access the divine wisdom, we reach a state of all-consciousness, one in which we know the answers to life's mysteries and our purpose in life.

The soul is not just a lofty goal pursued and obtained by philosophers and seekers; it exists for the everyday person to find, the person seeking to eke out a living for his or her family, the person trying to be a moral being in a challenging world, the person struggling to find meaning in chaos. The soul is nearer to us than we think and is aware of our day-to-day, mundane existence.

Often we are confused about why we are here and what is to be learned from our everyday existence. Whether we are aware of it or not, there is meaning to our life and all that happens to us. Whatever happens to us has a reason. If we could tap into our soul, we would see life as more than a string of meaningless events and would find a lesson and message in all that occurs.

Those who have tapped into their soul look at life from a refreshing perspective. Rather than be tossed about on the sea of life, dashed by every wave, they watch their life like a movie with subtitles, in which the words at the bottom of the screen let them know what is going on at the spiritual level. They may still experience the thrashing waves, but they observe them with the inner knowledge that there is reason and purpose to the particular situation.

We can look at all that happens to us through the eye of our immortal soul. When we do so, events become like passing, fleeting clouds upon the backdrop of a clear, calm, and peaceful sky. Our equanimity is preserved as we patiently wait for the fleeting events of life to cross our vision, knowing that one day they will be transformed into another scene, full of peace, joy, and love.

## ⊙ Activity ⊙

Take a moment to list all the things currently happening in your life. Think of the joys and sorrows. Think of all those confusing situations as well as joyful situations that cause you to ask, Why is this happening to me? After making this review, try the following activity:

Sit in a meditative mood. Make sure your environment is quiet, and that you are comfortable. Relax. Know that your soul is in tune with an unlimited wisdom within you. You are an ocean of all-knowingness. Everything that is known in the world flows from your ocean like rivulets. Now, observe your physical life through the eyes of unlimited wisdom. Observe the life situations that you listed above, but this time, be the empowered soul watching them like theater productions or movies. Consider that God the Parent and the empowered soul—its offspring—are in discussion about your life. Is there a higher angle from which to view your life? Listen to the answers that come from within you. As you learn the process of inversion or meditation, you will have a direct experience of true wisdom.

The voice of wisdom, cloaked by the ceaseless chattering of our mind, by the television, the world news, gossip and endless human conversations, has had no chance to communicate to us. Give it some time each day to speak to us. We should try to still our mind to hear our soul. Let us not confuse the mind's intellectual wrangling and endless analysis with the soul's wisdom. Let us learn to differentiate the two. When we listen to the wisdom of the soul, we can face the challenges of life with confidence and strength because we know the why's and wherefore's of all that happens.

##  What Is the Difference Between the Mind's Knowledge and the Soul's Wisdom?

As we practice listening to the empowered soul, we will begin to distinguish between the mind's knowledge and the soul's wisdom. Here are the basic differences between the two: the mind analyzes through the subjective eyes of the ego, while the soul views everything through the clear glass of truth. The ego is self-serving: What is in it for us? Will we get what we want? Will we gain power and control over others? The soul's truth is love, nonviolence, humility, purity, and selflessness. We can test any response we receive from within with this measuring stick. When the mind (ego) speaks, it aims to build us up, irrespective of the impact on others. Truth, however, aims for love and harmony. It asks, "How can I help others?" The mind and ego will stop at nothing to get what they want. They will resort to violence in thought, word, or deed; to greed, lust, anger, attachment, and selfishness. The empowered soul will give even of itself to walk the path of nonviolence, love, humility, self-lessness, and purity.

As we spend time daily in the silence of our soul and start to hear answers to the questions about our life, let us ask ourselves if the intent is coming from the mind and ego or from the soul, truth, and love. If we find that it is our ego and mind talking, let us go deeper until we find the answer from a place of love and truth. With practice, we can hear the inner whisperings of our soul's unlimited wisdom. We will find its guidance a source of strength and wisdom to guide our every step in life.

# *Immortality*  3

The soul is immortal; it knows no death. Yet many people fear death because they are not aware of their immortal nature. By connecting with our soul, we will have answers to what awaits us beyond death.

The world's main religions all recognize the immortality of the soul. The descriptions in the scriptures of the soul's journey after life differ from religion to religion, but one common thread runs throughout them: the soul survives the death of the physical body. Some people view this aspect of religion that deals with the soul's immortality as a hopeful wish, a fairy tale, or a pipe dream. Atheists may not believe in the soul or its immortality, agnostics may be unsure, and skeptics may question its validity, but all search for proof one way or the other.

The search to either prove or disprove the soul's immortal nature has been an ongoing quest for humanity through the ages. Evidence in support of the soul's immortality has appeared in two forms: The first consists of statements and accounts given by saints, prophets, and mystics who claimed to have passed through the gates of the Beyond in their mystic travels; the second consists of the accounts of people who have gone through near-death experiences—over eight million people in the past two decades have reported the occurrence in a similar manner.

##  How Do Various Traditions Describe the Soul's Immortality?

Ancient Egyptians believed that after death the soul lived on in an underworld region close to the earth. From this belief arose the ritual of burying the dead with their worldly possessions in case the dead needed them in the beyond. Massive pyramids and tombs were filled with not only the embalmed, mummified bodies of the dead, but also household objects, weapons, and jewelry. The Egyptians believed that the spirit, known as "ka," survived the body's physical death and remained near the earth, while a higher body, which kept the form and appearance it had on earth, ascended to more joyful regions, where it became one with Osiris, king of the world beyond.

Some early African societies also believed in the soul's immortality. They considered the dead to be as alive as the living. The dead lived somewhere between the earth and the spirits of those who were long departed, who lived in a more distant place. Sometimes the living would glimpse the spirit of the dead and would make them an offering of food or drink. They treated these spirits with respect, and they believed they could communicate with them.

In ancient Greece, people believed that the soul of a dead person was ferried across the dark waters of the river Styx. The soul then went to Hades where it was judged and assigned to a location according to the deeds it committed in life. Those who were to be punished were sent to Tartarus. Those who were to be rewarded went to the Elysian Fields, a place of gently blowing breezes filled with joy and bliss. Some souls were sent to Olympus to dwell forever with the immortal gods and goddesses.

The Greek philosophers Socrates and Plato also believed in the immortality of the soul. As Socrates told those around him before drinking the poison given to him by the authorities, "[When] I have drunk the poison I shall remain with you no longer, but depart to a state of heavenly happiness ..." In Socrates's teachings, he described how the soul was taken to a place of judgment after physical death. Souls who acted well in life went with a guide. Souls that were attached to the pleasures of the body hovered around the world for a long time and would be led away from this world only after much suffering. Those who lived a pure life of wisdom, love, and truth would go to a divine place to spend their time with God. Those whose lives were neither very good nor very bad went to a region in which they underwent purification for a time until their sins were absolved. Those who committed horrible deeds suffered in Tartarus until, at a later date, they would be forgiven by those they had hurt. If their crimes were so wicked they could not be forgiven, and they were not repentant, they would remain in Tartarus. Socrates also believed in the transmigration of the soul, in which a soul that was attached to the desires and pleasures of the physical world would return to a new body to continue life in this form.

The Greek "Mysteries" was a religion that passed on mystical secrets to its initiates. People from all over the ancient world including great philosophers and writers of the period journeyed to its center at Eleusis, near Athens, seeking initiation into the Mysteries. Members believed that a soul alternatively lived in a human body, then returned for some time to a radiant world of light, and then returned for another human birth. They believed that the light could appear as formless or it could take the shape of human form. They believed that death freed the soul from the prison of the physical world to inhabit a more beautiful, happier place. As long as the soul held on to earthly desires, it would return to the physical world. Once a soul achieved purity, it could live eternally in the higher worlds. Plato wrote, "In consequence of this divine initiation, we become spectators of entire, simple, immobile and blessed visions, resident in a pure light." (*Phaedrus*)

Hindus also believe in the immortality of the soul, which transmigrates from one life to another. The soul returns to life to work through its karmas, a collection of the thoughts, words, and deeds it experienced in its current and previous lives. Between each life, based on its deeds, the soul spends a specified amount of time in either heaven or hell. The soul then returns to earth for another life and a continuation of the cycle of birth and rebirth. It is only through salvation or *moksha* that a soul can be liberated from the continuing cycle of birth and death. Through spiritual practice and turning within, a soul can reach a state of communion with the Lord.

In the Book of Revelations in the New Testament, there is a description of the heavenly realms:

> *Then I saw a great white throne and Him who sat upon it; from His presence earth and sky fled away, and no place was found for them. And I saw the dead, great and small, standing before the throne, and books were opened. Also another book was opened, which is the book of life. And the dead were judged by what was written in the books, by what they had done.*
>
> (Revelations 20:11-12).

In Judaism, in the Mishnah, it is written:

> *Know also that everything is according to reckoning; and let not your imagination give you hope that the grave will be a place of refuge for you. For perforce you were formed, and perforce you were born, and perforce you live, and perforce you will die, and perforce you will in the future have to give account and reckoning before the King of kings, the Holy One, blessed is He.*
>
> (Mishnah, Abot 4:29).

There is also a description of the heaven region in the Talmud:

> Not like this world is the World to Come. In the World to Come there is neither eating nor drinking; no procreation of children or business transactions; no envy or hatred or rivalry; but the righteous sit enthroned, their crowns on their heads, and enjoy the luster of the Divine Splendor (Shechinah)."
>
> (Talmud, Berakot 17a).

The Muslims also believe in an afterlife for the soul. In the Qur'an it is written:

> You prefer this life, although the life to come is better and more enduring. All this is written in earlier scriptures; the scriptures of Abraham and Moses.
>
> (Qur'an 87.16-19)

According to the Muslims, the departing soul goes through a period of judgment; it can either go to heaven, hell, or ahraf, a place where there is neither pain nor pleasure.

The Jains have en entire cosmogony of regions of heavens and hells and spiritual worlds to which the soul travels in its journey.

Kabir Sahib of India gave a detailed account of the various planes of existence to which a soul goes after death. The three lower regions include the physical, astral, and causal regions that are made of mixtures of matter and consciousness and are subject to dissolution; the higher spiritual regions, which are eternal, include the supracausal plane and a spiritual plane known as Sach Khand or True Realm, from where God emanates. The soul transmigrates through a series of lives until it escapes the cycle. When it rises above the three lower planes, it is beyond the law of karma in which one is rewarded or punished for every thought, word, and deed. If it can rise above the three lower worlds, the soul enters the purely spiritual regions, where it merges with the Lord and lives eternally in bliss and love.

Guru Nanak and the Sikh Gurus also believed in the same journey of the soul after physical life. They spoke about having an account made of your deeds. The holy book of the Sikhs, the Adi Granth, gives an account of God's judgment process:

> *After you depart this life, God shall demand a reckoning of your*
>     *deeds*
> *That in His ledger are recorded.*
> *Those that are rebellious, shall be summoned.*
> *Azrael, the angel of death, will hover over them,*
> *And trapped in a blind alley they will know not any escape.*
> *Says Nanak, Falsehood must be destroyed;*
> *Truth in the end shall prevail.*
>
> (Adi Granth, Ramkali-ki-Var, M.1, p. 953)

The Jap Ji, written by Guru Nanak, gives an account of the higher regions beyond this world. The Sikhs believe that repetition of the five names of God (Panch Nama), as taught by their guru, is the way to escape the cycle of birth and rebirth and attain liberation or merging of the soul with the Divine. The Sufis also believe the soul is immortal and that repetition or *zikr* of the holy Names of God can liberate a soul and lead it to its reunion with God. Maulana Rumi describes the soul's journey as such:

> *I died as mineral and became a plant,*
> *I died as plant and rose to animal,*
> *I died as animal and I was a man.*
> *Why should I fear? When was I less by dying?*
> *Yet once more I shall die as man, to soar*
> *With angels blest; but even from angelhood*
> *I must pass on: all except God doth perish.*
> *When I have sacrificed my angel soul,*
> *I shall become what no mind e'er conceived,*
> *Oh, let me not exist! for Non-existence*
> *Proclaims in organ tones, 'To Him we shall return.'*
>
> (Thödol)

The Buddhist *Tibetan Book of the Dead*, or *Bardo Thödol* (*Liberation by Hearing on the After-Death Plane*), describes the immortality of the soul and its journey after death. It contains detailed instructions on how one can gain realization and thus escape the cycle of birth and death. The work is read at the time of death and serves as a guidepost for the departing spirit. The soul of the deceased spends some time in Bardo, close to the earth plane, where it witnesses scenes, both pleasant and terrifying, projected from the soul's conscious material. The reading of the book by the living, which is said to be heard by the soul in Bardo, guides the soul on how to react to each scene so that it does not become entrapped in what it sees. A reading from the book tells the soul to avoid getting lost in these scenes by concentrating on the "Clear Light of the Void" shining beyond the various scenes. By concentrating on the Light, the soul will achieve liberation from the cycle of rebirth and merge with the Source. If it cannot, the soul will pass through a judgment in which it reviews its karma from this life. The soul will then have to undergo the rewards or punishments for its deeds. It could go to a realm similar to an astral region for a period of time or it could go to one of the hell regions. A soul not liberated by absorption in the Light is thus lost in the cycle of the lower worlds or returns to earth for rebirth based on its karmas. The cycle continues until one escapes it with the help of an enlightened teacher who teaches the soul to remain absorbed in the radiant Light so it can transcend the lower regions and reach a state of nirvana, the spiritual abode.

Christian and Jewish mystics also speak of the soul's immortality and regions beyond this world. St. Teresa of Avila, St. Catherine of Sienna, St. John of the Cross, to name a few, had divine revelations that proved to them that the soul lives beyond this human existence.

In the Native American tradition, the Hopi believe that after death they join the spirits of loved ones who have already died as long as they live in a manner in which they keep their heart full of purity, showing kindness and generosity to others. Those who do not lead a good life are taken by witches, called "Two Hearts," and are led away to the country of the Two Hearts, which is filled with evil.

Theosophy, too, contains teachings about the immortality of the soul. In its cosmogony, there are various subplanes in the astral region, and the soul is placed in any one of the higher regions based on its life on earth. The lowest ones are reserved for criminals and people who committed evil. The intermediate subplanes are for people who sought worldly pleasures or were motivated by selfish desires. The highest subplanes are for intellectuals and religionists who were not particularly spiritual. Beyond the astral plane, Theosophists believe, is a mental plane where souls go when they leave their astral body. They call this plane and its seven subplanes Devachan. It is referred to as "heaven worlds." The four lowest planes are the mental plane, and the three highest subplanes are the causal plane. These regions are said to be beyond anything that we know on earth and cannot be adequately described in any language or terms that that the human brain can understand. They are regions of bliss and knowledge, a reward for the soul's good deeds. The ultimate stage, according to Theosophists, is nirvana or union with the Lord. The souls that continue in the cycle of birth and death must pass through a stage of forgetfulness to erase memories of their sojourn through the inner regions before they return to the earth life.

These accounts of the soul's immortality are not coincidental. There is a truth behind the revelations of all the saints, mystics, prophets, and enlightened ones who have come through the ages. The question now is whether there is any evidence that can be confirmed today by modern science to validate the findings of the religious founders of the past.

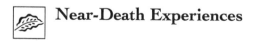 **Near-Death Experiences**

A new field of study that has arisen since the 1970's seems to bear out some of the accounts left to us by the past saints and spiritual teachers. A medical doctor, Dr. Raymond Moody, Jr., discovered that those patients who had clinically died but were brought back to life through the wonders of modern medicine all had a similar experience. Many of them reported finding themselves looking down at their body from a vantage point in the room such as the ceiling. They were able to watch the medical practitioners trying to bring them back to life, and they could hear conversations in the room. Some found themselves floating through walls to the waiting room where they could see and hear their relatives, and later, after the patient was revived, relatives and friends confirmed the accuracy of the overheard conversations. The subjects then found themselves being sucked through a dark tunnel, at the end of which was a bright light. Although the light was extremely bright, brighter than any they had ever seen on earth, it was not scorching; rather, it was a warm light, which they described as being filled with love. Many of them were met by a Being of Light who enveloped them with a love greater than they ever felt on earth. Following this, many went through a life review in which everything they had done in their life flashed before them. They could see not only the event, but could experience what they and the other people involved thought and felt. Thus, if they did something hurtful, they could feel the pain they caused the other person. If they did something loving, they could feel the happiness of the other person. As a result of this life review, most people underwent a transformation. They realized that when they crossed the borders to the afterlife, it did not matter how much money they earned, how much property they had owned, what position of power they had held, or whether they were famous or not; what mattered was how loving they were to others. Love was the most important measure of the value of the life they led. Thus, when they returned to their body and resumed life, they were often changed. In many cases, they began to devote themselves to being a more loving, caring, and kind person to those around them. They also spoke of being given a choice of whether they wanted to remain in the life beyond or return. Many of them experienced so much bliss in the beyond that they did not want to return. But, ultimately, they were told that their life on earth was not over and they would have to return. At that point, they found themselves being sucked back into their body. At that moment, any medical efforts to revive them bore fruit, and their heartbeat and breathing suddenly resumed.

As mentioned previously, over eight million people reported having a near-death experience, according to a 1982 Gallup poll. The startling number has caused many doctors and scientists to take notice. Dr. Raymond Moody's book *Life After Life*, and Dr. Melvin Morse's work with the near-death experiences of children, have given public awareness to this phenomena. As a result of their work, many people who had had such experiences but were hesitant to talk about them out of fear of ridicule, were now given courage to voice their experiences. The media has responded as well, and there have been many books, television programs, seminars, and even movies about these experiences.

Do near-death experiences prove the existence of the soul? They are proof to the people who have had them. Their accounts attest passionately to the existence of a life beyond; in fact, many say the experiences had a vividness more real than their earthly life. Confirmation of conversations they overhead in rooms other than where the dying person lay, even the conversations of relatives in other states to whom the soul apparently journeyed for a visit, erased doubts in the person having the experience that the soul exists, and even caused the relatives involved to be convinced of this as well.

##  How Can We Experience the Soul's Immortality?

There is also a striking similarity among the accounts of the journey of the soul as related by enlightened ones from different world religions. The common thread among them is the belief that the soul lives after the demise of the physical body, undergoes a judgment in which its good and bad deeds are either rewarded or punished, is placed in heaven or hell according to its deeds, and ultimately reaches a stage of union with the Lord or the Source. There is also a similarity between these and the accounts of people who have had a near-death experience. Their descriptions seem to correspond with the scriptures that describe initial moments when one's soul departs from the body. The near-death experiences take us as far as the threshold of the inner realms. But since the narrators did not permanently die, their journey ended there.

Although the accounts of saints and those alive today who have had near-death experiences may give us hope and inspiration, they alone cannot provide proof to our selves. They represent merely secondhand knowledge. The real proof comes when we experience our soul's immortality for ourselves.

We need not experience the trauma of a near-death experience in order to find out what lies beyond; we can experience the soul's immortal nature when we go within. We can learn how to do this by examining how the saints and mystics from all different religions conducted their inner journey. We can learn the techniques they used and begin to practice them ourselves. Later in the book, some techniques will be given to help us get started on the journey within.

## ∞ **Activity** ∞

Sit in a relaxed, meditative state. Try to forget about your body, and try to still your thoughts. Sit in a state of just being. What part of you is conscious when your mind and body are still? Let go of all your tensions and problems. Learn to spend some time each day just being. Later, as you learn the meditation techniques, you will become experienced with sitting in a state of quietude, which will prepare you for experiencing the empowered soul within.

∞

# *Unconditional Love* 4

We seek to love and be loved. During our life's journey we may go through many relationships in search of the perfect love. We want a love that will fill us with warmth and joy. We desire a love in which we will be accepted for who we are despite our faults. We want a love that will not leave us. We want a love that will last forever.

Throughout our life we experience many relationships. There are those of parent and child, brothers and sisters, friends, lovers, and spouses. We want fulfillment in each of these relationships, and we are disappointed if something goes wrong with them. We have expectations that the love between us will manifest in a particular way and are disappointed when these expectations are not met. While we rise above the challenges in some relationships to form a stronger bond, in others we break off the relationship.

Even if we find a wonderful relationship with someone, we may have to suffer the loss of our loved one through illness, separation, or death.

We may wonder, Is there any love that is permanent? Is there a love that knows no separation and no end?

The answer is yes. There is a permanent, lasting love in the empowered soul. There is an unconditional love waiting for us within. Connecting with that love envelops us in warmth, joy, and ecstasy.

##  Is There a Love Greater than Any in This World?

Loving relationships reflect the love of the empowered soul. One of the greatest loves we know in this world is that of the parent for a child. If we were lucky enough to experience the love of our parents, we may recall how much they cared for us. They worked hard to earn money for our food, clothing, shelter, medicine, education, and toys. They spent great amounts of time nurturing us. If we were on a sports team, they may have watched us play. If we were in a school performance, they may have taken time to attend. Even if we did not have a loving relationship, our mother still carried us in her womb for nine months and underwent the birth pangs to bring us into the world.

In our adult life we may have experienced a romantic love. We may have found ourselves falling in love with someone and becoming lost in the intoxication of that love. We may have felt that all the problems of the world and our worries disappeared in the company of our loved one. Time seemed to fly and we could have been lost for hours in conversation with that person or in looking into each other's eyes. The romantic love made us blind to each other's imperfections and faults.

If later in life we became parents, we experienced another kind of love. We may have been overwhelmed by the feeling of love as we held our baby in our arms and looked into his or her eyes. The tiny fingers wrapped around our hand may have filled us with an indescribable sense of warmth. We finally may have come to realize how much love our parents felt for us. No sacrifice was too great to make sure our child had the best food, clothing, and toys.

These outer loves are but a small reflection of the great love that exists in our soul. If we multiply the greatest love we have known in this outer world by tenfold or a hundredfold, we may have some inkling of the love that awaits us within.

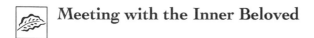 ## Meeting with the Inner Beloved

Read any account of a near-death experience and you get a glimpse into the great love awaiting us within. Many of them describe a meeting with a Being of Light, from whom they felt more love than they ever felt on earth. It was an all-embracing love that enraptured every pore of their being. The recipient of that love was filled with a divine sweetness and intoxication that they did not want to give up. The Being of Light may have helped the person go through a life review of all the good and bad deeds. Yet, no matter how bad someone was, the Being of Light still overwhelmed the person with unconditional love. For the first time in the person's life, he or she felt loved to the very core of his or her being.

Although the love of the Being of Light is greater than what many people ever feel on earth, that too, is but a portion of an even greater love—the love of God. God's love is beyond imagination. The Being of Light's love is a drop of God's love. The soul is a drop of that same love. That spark of God within each of us is love personified. Its very nature is love. We carry that infinite love within us.

How do we know about the immensity of that love? Every saint, mystic, prophet, and enlightened soul speaks of God's love. Read the words of Christ, Mohammed, Buddha, Mahavira, Guru Nanak, Kabir, Mira Bai, Rabia Basri, Baba Farid, St. Teresa of Avila, St. John of the Cross, and numerous others and you will find descriptions of the unconditional love we can access by realizing our soul.

The Sufis refer to God as the Beloved. Much of mystic poetry and scriptural text uses the terminology of the lover and Beloved to describe the soul and God. While it appears that they are two entities, the lover and the Beloved, the final revelatory moment uncovers that they are one and the same. The soul and God are, in essence, one. The journey of discovery leads the soul from believing it is separate from God to its ultimate enlightenment when it realizes that it is one with God. The mystic journey is the story of the separation of the soul from God and its final communion. Thus, if we tap into our empowered soul, we are actually diving into the ocean of the Lord's love.

St. Catherine of Siena, a Christian saint, provides us with a vision of her mystic marriage. From childhood, she had been blessed with many divine inner visions, one of which told her that she was betrothed to the Lord. In 1366, a voice said to her, "Today I will celebrate solemnly with you the feast of the betrothal of your soul, and even as I promised I will espouse you to Myself in faith." She then saw a vision in which the Virgin Mother took Catherine's right hand, and held it out to Christ to wed her to Him.

Christ then took out a gold ring with four pearls surrounding a beautiful diamond. He placed the ring upon Catherine's finger and said, "I wed you to Myself. " He instructed her to do those works which He would put in her hands. He told her that she was now filled with the fortitude of faith and would happily overcome all adversaries. The vision disappeared, but from that day onward St. Catherine saw the ring on her finger.

A fourteenth-century German Dominican mystic, Suso, a disciple of Meister Eckhart, was also blessed with visions of the Lord. In one, he described how he found himself surrounded by heavenly spirits. He asked one of the most luminous of them, "Show me how God dwells in my soul."

The angel told him, "Do but fix your eyes joyously upon yourself, and watch how God plays the game of love within your loving soul." Suso looked quickly and saw that the heart region of his body was pure and transparent like crystal. He saw divine wisdom peacefully enthroned in the middle of his heart. Next to divine wisdom was the soul resting lovingly on God's bosom. God was embracing him and pressing him to

His heart. His soul remained absorbed and intoxicated with love in the arms of God.[1]

In Sufism, we have the words of Jalaluddin Rumi in his "Festival of Spring":

> *With Thy Sweet Soul, this soul of mine*
> *Hath mixed as Water doth with Wine.*
> *How can the Wine and Water part,*
> *Or me and Thee when we combine?*
> *Thou art become my greater self;*
> *Small bounds no more can me confine,*
> *Thou hast my being taken on,*
> *And shall not I now take on Thine?*
> *Me Thou for ever hast affirmed,*
> *That I may ever know Thee mine.*
> *Thy Love has pierced me through and through,*
> *Its thrill with Bone and Nerve entwine.*
> *I rest a Flute laid on Thy lips;*
> *A lute, I on Thy breast recline.*
> *Breathe deep in me that I may sigh;*
> *Yet strike my strings, and tears shall shine.*[2]

Human language fails to adequately describe the inner meeting of the soul with its Source, therefore mystics and saints have had to rely heavily on the closest analogy they could find, the communion of the lover and Beloved. It is a meeting that enraptures the soul, filling it with exquisite intoxication that permeates every part of its being.

 ## Intoxication of Love

Oftentimes, the rapture of love that the soul experiences is so great it causes one to enter a state known as the madness of love. The soul is enflamed with an endless, burning desire for union with the Beloved. Any separation is as painful as a knife cutting the heart into two. The mystic poet–saint, Sant Darshan Singh, has written thousands of verses, such as the following one, on the state of all-encompassing love between the soul and God:

> *I have no friend except my Beloved,*
> *I have no work except his love.*

Just as a lover is absorbed day and night with thoughts of its beloved, the soul becomes caught in that state after its first taste of union with the Lord and the Lord's permeating love.

On the bliss of being with the Beloved within, Sant Darshan Singh writes:

> *Wherever I traveled*
> *From earth to the milky way,*
> *I met love at every step*
> *And beauty in every glance.*

When we are in love, the world and our life become beautified. Everything takes on a vividness and richness unseen before. One's world undergoes a transformative beauty in the presence of the Beloved. As Sant Darshan Singh says:

> *The autumn-stricken paths suddenly bloomed and blossomed,*
> *In whatever direction the Beloved turns, there is only spring.*

What is it like for the soul to be lost in love with its Beloved Lord? It is more beautiful than being with your beloved in gardens landscaped with dancing fountains surrounded by a myriad of fragrant flowers. It is lovelier than sitting together on a hillside watching the brilliant colors of a setting sun. It is more peaceful than sitting by a gently flowing stream in a cool forest. It is more uplifting than the haunting violin and the angelic harps. It is like being permeated from head to toe with divine love.

##  Soul Loves All Unconditionally

Along with the intoxication and madness of this love comes another aspect: This love is unconditional. It knows no discrimination, no prejudice, and no separatism. Our soul is loved unconditionally by the Lord. We, in turn, can reflect that love and radiate unconditional love to those we meet.

There are few examples of unconditional love in our everyday relationships. In examples of the greatest love relationships in the world, there always seem to be some conditions placed on them. In the parent's love for a child, there are expectations. The parent may want the child to behave a certain way. When the child grows up and the parent grows old, there may be expectations that the child will care for the parent. Thus, the love is not entirely unconditional. In the love between lovers and spouses, there is always some expectation that the lover will make us happy. We want the lover to provide us with the fulfillment we seek. If the lover's behavior does not meet our expectations we may argue and fight, and in some cases even break up.

The soul loves unconditionally, because God loves unconditionally. The soul and God are one and the same. If we tap into our soul and look at the world through its eyes, we can not only love unconditionally, but also feel God's unconditional love for us. The sun does not discriminate as to which flowers it will shine upon. It sheds its light on all equally. Thus, roses and violets, tulips and weeds all receive the same light. So it is with God's love. It shines on us all, whether we are man or woman, Hindu or Muslim, Christian or Jew, Sikh or Sufi, Parsi or Jain. It shines on us no matter what color our hair, skin, or eyes. When we experience our soul and begin to identify with it, we too can grow in our love of all people.

St. Francis of Assisi is best known for his love for all living things. It is said, however, that early in his life he had difficulty dealing with his feelings toward lepers. He dreaded them and shirked away from them when they were near. One day, as he was walking down the road, a leper came into his path. His first reaction was to turn in the other direction. He was sickened not so much by the sight of the leper but by his own inability to love the person. He knew that he was not representing God's unconditional love in shunning the afflicted man. In an attempt to overcome this weakness, he walked up to the leper, embraced him, and kissed him on his neck. Filled with God's love, he then continued on his way. When he turned to look back at the leper, he saw there was no one in sight. He realized that God had come to him in the form of the leper to test him, and he had passed his lesson. St. Francis had looked at the leper through the heart of his empowered soul, and from that day on, he ministered to the lepers and all others afflicted with illness through the love of God in his heart.

One of the most powerful illustrations of unconditional love is found in the teachings of Christ. The foundation of Christianity is based on the concept of love and forgiveness. As Christ said, "Ye have heard that it hath been said, thou shalt love thy neighbor and hate thine enemy. But I say unto you, love your enemies, bless them that curse you, do good to them that hate you, and pray for them which despitefully use you, and persecute you (Matt. 5:43, 44).

The world is in need of unconditional love. Just as we wish to be loved unconditionally, so too can we love those around us unconditionally.

True love means loving everyone. Saints and mystics point out that if we truly love God, we will love all God's children. As Christ said, "If anyone says, 'I love God,' and hates his brother, he is a liar; for he who does not love his brother whom he has seen, cannot love God whom he has not seen" (1 John 4.7-20).

When we tap into our empowered soul, we can become blind to outer differences of religion, culture, color, and nationality. All can be seen as one family of God, and we can learn to channel the love of our empowered soul to all we meet.

 ## Seeing Love Everywhere

The soul recognizes its own nature of love in every living creature and in all life itself. As Sant Darshan Singh wrote:

*He is hidden in every instrument, in every song and melody.*
*All creation reflect His glory.*
*There exists not a sparkling wave nor a fiery star*
*    that does not owe its radiance to His Light.*

Maulana Rumi has said, "The current of love from the one God is flowing through the entire universe. What do you think when you look at the face of a person? Look at him carefully. He is not a person, but a current of the essence of God, which permeates him."

Lord Krishna said, "He who is able to see My form in everything, who realizes that there is no difference between different beings is, in fact, the true seer. Such a person I can never forget."

 ## Seek the Love Within

How can we find the intoxicating love of our empowered soul? It is not in the stars, or on the mountaintops, or deep under the sea. It is within us. Kabir Sahib said:

*Within his navel the musk is hid, the bewildered deer hunts for it*
*    in the forest.*
*So also dwells the Beloved within the heart,*
*    yet the world knows it not and seeks Him outside itself.*

We look for fulfillment in the outer loves of this world, which may give us transient joy for a while. Yet, we can also have a permanent joy alongside our outer loves. We can experience the love of our empowered soul. This love will not take away from our outer loves; rather, it will enrich them. We will still love our family, our spouse, and our friends. The difference is that by tapping into our soul's state of unconditional love, we can receive all the fulfillment and intoxication we desire. We no longer have to depend on anyone else to meet our expectations. We can be satisfied from within and not dependent on another for joy. Instead, we will pour out our love unconditionally. Instead of seeking to take love, we can give love. By doing so, we will find that our relationships are smoother, more harmonious, and more peaceful. The tension and anxiety that come from trying to get another person to meet our needs can vanish like a passing cloud. Instead, we can be fulfilled from within and be free to enjoy a richness to our relationships.

## ∽ **Activity** ∾

Sit in a state of meditation. Relax. Think of someone you love whose memory fills you with peace, joy, and happiness. Experience that love within for a while. Now, extend that love to others. Radiate that love to other family members, friends, and co-workers. Extend it further to other people in your life. Extend it to a person, a group of people, another cultural group, another religious group, or a group of people from another nation. With practice, you can become in tune with how your soul loves the world. In a final exercise, let this love engulf the entire planet.

∽

# *Fearlessness* 5

Fearlessness is a quality of the empowered soul. Our soul lives in a perpetual state without fear. It is the source of all power and knows no fear. By tapping our soul, we can access this state of fearlessness so that we can face our fears and problems with renewed confidence, trust, and security.

We all face moments that challenge even the strongest of men and women. We may be in an accident that debilitates us, making us weak and helpless. We may find that our child has contracted a serious illness and as they cry out for us to help them we feel powerless to relieve his or her pain. We may give birth to a child that has a mental challenge that requires all our patience and courage to help him or her through life. A loved one receives news that he or she has a terminal disease, and we must stand by his or her side through the final days. A fire, flood, or tornado destroys our home and all our belongings. The company to whom we gave thirty years of work is downsizing, and we are let go, uncertain of what new career to pursue. Few people pass through life without the challenge of facing some affliction.

The parable of the mustard seed illustrates that no matter how comfortable we may currently be, we cannot expect to pass through the obstacle course of life without some challenge that requires courage. A woman once came to Lord Buddha crying bitterly that her only son had passed away. Holding the dead body of her child in her arms, she begged Buddha to restore the youth to life. Buddha, in his wisdom, explained to her lovingly that it could not be done. Life is transitory and sooner or later we all must die, he told her. Stubbornly refusing to accept his answer, the woman pleaded with him passionately to perform a miracle and bring her son back to life.

Buddha finally gave in and told her, "All right, I will restore your son to life on one condition."

"What is that?" asked the woman.

"I will do so only on the condition that you bring to me the mustard seed from a home in which the family has not seen any death."

Heartened by the hope that this would be an easy task, the woman set off in search of the mustard seed. When she reached the first home, she knocked on the door and a couple answered.

"What can we do for you?" they asked.

"My son has just died, and Lord Buddha has agreed to bring him back to life if I could bring him a mustard seed from the home of a family who has seen no death."

The woman of the house, sympathetic but also frustrated, said, "We have just lost our father several weeks ago, our crops are failing, and we have not enough to feed our children. We are sorry for your loss, but you have come to the wrong house."

The woman thanked them and went on to the next house. She spent the day going from house to house, discovering that all her neighbors were beset by some calamity or sorrow or another. For several days she continued her search. There was not one home that did not have a tale of woe to tell. Exhausted, she returned to Lord Buddha empty-handed. She realized that no one was exempt from pain at one time or another, and that her son's death was an inevitable part of life.

## Challenges Are a Part of Life

Many of us are unprepared for life's challenges. We often find that during those times we crack under its pressures. We may cheerfully care for loved ones who are ill for the first few days or weeks, but as their illness lingers and we find no change in their progress, we may feel that the strains of life begin to threaten our equanimity and patience.

Ongoing problems and setbacks often take their toll on us. If we lose our job, we may feel encouraged for the first few weeks that we will find a better job quickly, but after months of searching fruitlessly we may become depressed and hopeless. A child who gets a poor grade once in a while may disappoint us, but if the same child continues to do poorly in school year after year it causes us discouragement and frustration.

Our search for a spouse may make us anxious, but if, after years, we still do not find the perfect mate, we may develop anxiety with all its physical symptoms. On the other hand, those who are in a failing marriage and seeking a separation, go through the pain of loss and all its stresses as well.

We cannot put an end to life's challenges. We have no control over the outer universe. We cannot say for certain that we will not lose our job, our home, our wealth, or a loved one. We cannot prevent a hurricane, volcano, earthquake, tidal wave, or tornado from bringing destruction. We cannot prevent the inevitable end to our physical life. What we can do is face these challenges with a sense of fearlessness so that we are not incapacitated by fear and despair.

## Why Do We Have Fear?

Fear arises from doubt and from the unknown. When we have doubts about how something is going to turn out, it opens the door to fear. When we doubt ourselves, we fear making a wrong decision or making a mistake. If we doubt our abilities, we fear that we will fail in a competition or a test. When we doubt whether an outcome will turn out right, we fear the consequences. If we doubt the existence of a controlling power, we live in fear of chance occurrences and accidents.

Untruth also leads to fear. If we tell a lie, we live in fear of being caught. We must create an intricate web of lies to cover the first lie. The number of lies becomes so great that it is hard to track what we said to whom and when we said it. Rather than bringing closure to the situation by telling the truth, we spend weeks, months, and even years spinning yarns to cover up the initial lie. Fear grips us any time someone comes close to knowing the truth, for then we will be exposed and must pay the consequences of the deed we were trying to hide.

We fear being weak. The young boy or girl on the school playground fears the bully. Each day as he or she walks home from school, the weak child lives in fear of being physically attacked by the bigger children. At work, the employee fears the employer. The employer holds the future of our salary and job in his or her hands. We may feel weak and powerless to speak up for injustices on the job because those who hold the power may retaliate and punish us for doing so.

If we examine our lives, we find that we are fearful of many things. As children, we fear and worry about how long our parents are going to be there to support us. As students, we live in fear of failing our examinations. As parents, we fear whether or not our child is going to be healthy or whether or not he or she will grow to be a good person. As business owners, we worry about whether our competitors are getting the better of us. Each one of us is fearful about one aspect of our life or another. Behind all these fears is the fear that is at the heart of each of us, and that is fear of the unknown.

Lord Mountbatten, the last British viceroy and governor-general of India before India received its independence, used to fear the dark as a child. He was hesitant to go to bed alone. When his father asked him what he was afraid of, little Louis Mountbatten replied, "I am not afraid of the dark. I am afraid of the wolves here." When his father replied, "There are no wolves in the house," the child responded, "I daresay there aren't, but I think there are!"

We are more afraid of our thoughts of what is out there than of what is actually out there. Those who fear death, in actuality, fear the unknown. We all know that one day we are going to die. Many believe that the annihilation of ourselves is the end of our existence. That fear is always trying to eat us up in one manner or another. People fear the unknown because it may be unpleasant or painful. Since they do not know what to expect, anxiety and fear builds within them. There are many people who do believe in life after death. What they fear then is the unknown of how they are going to die and what they will experience at the time of death. They fear the pain of death. Fear of the unknown runs like a continuous thread in the back of our minds throughout our life.

 ## Soul's Fearlessness

Our soul, which is totally conscious, is a part of God and, therefore, is without fear. Since God is all-consciousness, and the soul is one with the Lord, it is God in a microcosm. God is without fear, and the soul is also without fear. It is only when we are out of touch with our soul that we begin to be afraid. The soul is truth; the soul is totally conscious. Being in connection with absolute truth means there is no fear. Thus, there is no fear in the soul.

The soul's quality of wisdom gives it access to the knowledge of all that is. There is nothing potentially unknown to the soul. It knows what is and what is to be. What has it to fear? Those who have been in touch with their soul—the saints, mystics, prophets, and enlightened beings—have come to understand the process of death through firsthand experience. This knowledge helps eliminate the fear of death.

The saints tell us that what dies is the physical body, which is made of matter. Being made of matter, it deteriorates, it decays, and is finally destroyed. But our true self, which is our spirit or soul, is eternal. It lives on and on and on. What we call death in this world of ours is only a physical death. For the soul, it is just the changing of a vesture. Therefore, the first thing to understand is that our soul is everlasting. It existed in the beginning, it exists now, and it will always exist. There is no question of the destruction of the soul; it is eternal. If we can realize this for ourselves, one of the greatest fears of our life, the unknown nature of death, will be eliminated.

##  Truth Knows No Fear

The soul is truth. Untruth lives in fear of being exposed. But as Mahatma Gandhi often said, "Truth always wins in the end." Truth conquers all. If we live in truth, we have nothing to fear.

We may not want to recognize it, but there are laws by which the universe is governed. Ignorance of the laws is no excuse. We may think we can get away with deceiving others, with deceiving ourselves, with deceiving God, but we cannot get away with these acts. Sooner or later truth is revealed, and the consequences of our actions must be paid.

If we read the newspapers, we find thieves may rob a bank and get away. Parents lie to their children, and children lie to their parents. We may take money that is not ours from our place of employment. We may cheat on our loved ones. We may pretend to have power that we do not have in order to get people to do what we want. We manipulate others to get our way. We make promises we have no intention of keeping. There are numerous shades of untruths in which human beings are involved. But in the end the truth will catch up with us, if not in this life, then on our day of judgment. No matter what religion we follow, there is accountability for our doings. The description of the form in which this day of reckoning comes may vary according to the teachings of different religions, but all the different accounts stem from one truth: there is a day of reckoning for each of us.

Living in truth frees us from fear. We neither fear having to account for untruth, nor fear being found out. The prisoner who has served time in jail for wrongdoings based on lies, deception, and dishonesty decides to live a clean life of truth. How freeing it is for that criminal to wake up each day and enjoy life without looking over his or her shoulder in fear of getting caught. The person who speeds on the highway is always tense, wondering whether the police will stop him or her for a traffic violation. The driver can neither enjoy the scenery or the conversation in the car. But the person who drives at the posted speed limit does not have to drive in fear. That person can enjoy the sights along the way, the music on the radio, or the discussions with other passengers without fear hanging over his or her head.

The soul's existence is truth. If we can tap into the soul, then our real nature as truth will govern our lives and free us from fear.

 ## Becoming Desensitized

In medicine, to desensitize someone is to give one small doses of the substance to which one is allergic. By learning to tolerate small doses, the body builds resistance and can handle larger doses of the irritating substance. If we begin to practice fearlessness in small situations, we can grow in our ability to handle greater and greater challenges. To practice fearlessness we must come in contact with our empowered soul.

## ∞ Activity ∞

Make a list of all the things you fear. Try to analyze your fears by finding their root cause and placing them in categories. Which fears are based on doubt or on living in untruth? Which are based on fear of the unknown? After doing this, pick one of the lesser fears you have.

Begin the process of desensitization by eliminating one of your lesser fears. The following activity may help.

Sit in a meditative way and relax. You are going to face your fear, but you will not do it alone. You are going to approach it as the empowered soul who is one with God. The empowered soul and God have no fear. They are fearless. If you were to relive the fear you have selected to examine from the perspective of your empowered soul, you would know that the situation cannot hurt you. Your empowered soul, being one with God, is strong and powerful. It is stronger than that which you fear. Your fears dissipate when confronted by your empowered soul.

Know that your empowered soul is the one who is really facing your challenges. If you connect with your empowered soul, you will overcome all fears and gain a lasting sense of peace and security.

∞

In this connection, there is a story about a man who was being chased by a ferocious lion. To his horror, the man found himself at the edge of a cliff with nowhere to turn. Seeing a branch below, he had no alternative but to jump off the cliff and catch hold of the branch, thus escaping the lion. Believing he would remain on the branch until the lion left, he was mortified to find that a small mouse was eating away at the tree limb. He looked down and saw that the valley was thousands of feet below. There he was with the lion above him and the long fall below him. Not knowing what to do, he prayed to God for help. "I'll do anything you ask, if You can just help me!" pleaded the man. The man was startled to hear the voice of God speak to him. God said, "You will do anything I ask?" "Yes, God, just please save me!" "Okay," said God.

"Let go of the branch and I will save you." The man thought for a moment and said, "Is there anyone else up there I can talk to but You?"

We, too, want God to rescue us, but we will not let go and trust in God. Our empowered soul, being one with God, is there for us. It is there to help us through the challenges of life. We just need to let go of our ego and intellect and let the fearless soul face our challenges for us. We will find that our lives will be filled with safety, security, confidence, and trust, and we will be free to walk our path free of fear.

# Connectedness  6

People around the world were excited when the personal computer became accessible to consumers so that they could store and process information. But in the last few years, technology has taken a still greater leap. Using a small computer on a desk at home, or a portable laptop, we can now connect with all available knowledge on other computers. A computer can now link us to the latest news, stock reports, airline ticket agents, home shopping, the latest medical breakthroughs, and information in every sphere of knowledge.

The connectedness to information that we experience with computers is a small sample of the powerful connections we can make with our empowered soul. The empowered soul experiences universal connection with all beings. Becoming aware of this unifying force can help us realize our essential unity.

## Overcoming Separateness

Walls of division separate people. If we are born in one part of the world we say, "I am a citizen of this country, or that country." If we are born into a certain religion, we say, "I am a follower of such and such religion." Religions are man-made. There was no Buddhism before Buddha. There was no Christianity before Jesus. It was the followers of the great saints, mystics, and prophets who organized their teachings into a religion.

Most often, we become a member of a religion based on our parents' beliefs. A Hindu infant who is orphaned as an infant and adopted by a Christian may become Christian. Similarly, if we are born in a certain state or country, we live in the way dictated by the customs of that region. For example, many people worship God through prayer. But the way they pray differs between cultures. Quite often, practices are influenced by geographical factors. For example, in countries where water is plentiful, people may wash their hands before praying. But in desert countries where water is scarce, rubbing one's hands in sand may become part of the religious custom. Similarly, in some warm climates, it is customary to remove shoes before entering a holy place; yet in colder climates, going barefoot may be impractical. Over time, customs that originate for climatic reasons become sanctified and made part of the religious law. Instead of being tolerant of other religions with different customs, people use those differences as a basis for prejudice and hatred.

Another dividing factor is language. When people in different religions use different words for the same concept, it becomes an excuse for thinking the other religion is not as good as one's own. For example, each religion has its own name for God, based on the language or culture in which the religion originated. God is named Allah by the Muslims, Wah-i-guru by the Sikhs, Paramatma by the Hindus, God or the Lord by the Christians and the Jews. No matter the language, the words all refer to the same God. Yet we make these language differences a source of contention and separation. What we forget is that God existed before language was created.

As human beings, we put boundaries around ourselves, and in the process, we limit ourselves. But our soul is limitless. Behind the divisions that we create on the physical plane, is a unifying force connecting all life. The truth that the great saints and mystics tried to convey was that we are all a part of God. We are soul. We are conscious. We are full of the love of God. It is only at the human level that we make divisions. The soul is a part of God, the Creator. For us to be able to truly understand ourselves, we need to recognize all the divisions as walls that surround our true self. These walls are keeping us away from truth. These walls need to be brought down in order for us to truly understand the oneness of all life. Sant Darshan Singh has said it in verse:

> *What does it matter if I am called a man,*
> *In truth, I am the very soul of love.*
> *The entire earth is my home,*
> *And the universe my country.*

Through lack of self-knowledge, we create separation. Through our soul, we can experience connectedness and create more peace and harmony among the inhabitants of this planet.

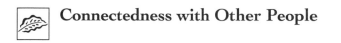 ## Connectedness with Other People

The soul is light and love. If we could look down on humanity from a higher vantage point we would see a light illuminating each soul, just as when we fly in an airplane at night and look down at the earth we see a myriad of lights. The light in each soul is one and the same. God sees no distinction in any of the lights because they are all made of the same essence as the Creator. What differs is but the outer human form surrounding it. When we realize our soul, we attain the same consciousness as God.

Within our outer forms is the soul. This means that at our core we are not different. We are all love, we are all consciousness, we are all light, we are all immortality. This makes us, in effect, part of one family. When asked what race we are, each one of us should reply we are part of the human race.

Let us think of our parents. One generation before them were two sets of people who produced our two parents. One generation before them were eight people who produced those four. A generation before them were sixteen people. If we go back far enough, we will find that the human population was small, and that at some point we were all connected by the same ancestors. If we build a human family tree over centuries, we will find that we are truly long-lost cousins to each other. Who is the stranger then? No one. We are all brothers and sisters of the universal family. If we could only treat all human beings in this way, there would be no question of divisions based on outer differences.

There is such joy in feeling connected with people. How rich our day would be if we went around smiling and saying hello to people we met rather than walking by as strangers. By taking a moment and saying something nice to our co-workers, the postal carrier, the shopkeeper, the bus driver, the elevator attendant, and the garbage collector as if they were our friends or relatives, we would make someone else's day special. Words cannot describe the internal joy we receive from making someone else happy.

It is said that it is better to give than to receive. Why? In giving, our heart expands. When we are kind, we put ourselves in touch with God. When we feel connected to other people, we connect ourselves to the Lord.

This calls to mind the story of Abou Ben Adhem. He was a good man who loved his fellow beings. One night he was awakened by an angel, who was sitting and writing something in a large book.

"What are you writing?" inquired Abou Ben Adhem.

The angel replied, "I am writing the names of those who love the Lord."

"Is my name there?" asked Abou Ben Adhem.

The angel checked and said, "No, I do not see it here."

To which Abou Ben Adhem replied, "Please list me as one who loves his fellow man." The angel did so, and then disappeared.

The following night, the angel returned, opened the book, and showed Abou Ben Adhem his name. The angel explained, "I have spoken to God and God has placed your name at the top of the list of those who loved God."

By loving his fellow human beings, Abou Ben Adhem was, in fact, loving God. Those who love their fellow human beings are the true lovers of God.

## Connectedness with Animals

Those truly connected with God feel a love for all creatures, great and small. The light of God illumines all life forms. It is as much present in the ant as it is in the lion or the fish or the birds. We can witness the flaming glory of God when we look at life through the eyes of the soul. With that perspective, we can develop love for all.

The following is an account illustrating the universality of love that saints have even for animals. Sain, a saint from India, was preparing a meal of flat bread, called chapati. A dog entered his room and snatched the chapati and ran out. Sain ran after him as onlookers observed.

"Look at him chasing that dog over a mere chapati," they remarked.

But the crowd was amazed when they heard Sain cry out to the dog, "Wait. Let me put butter on your bread for you as well!" To Sain, the dog had entered his home like the best of guests, and just as one would naturally serve the guest a buttered chapati, so, too, did Sain wish to treat his canine guest in a hospitable manner.

The Jain tradition promotes a great respect for all life forms. The reason that Jains wear a mask around their faces is so as not to breathe in any living organisms that inhabit the air and thereby cause their death. They sweep the streets in front of them before they take a step, lest they tread on a small insect.

Our soul treads softly over the soil of life. It has the ability to recognize God in all living creatures and would not take the life of any of God's children. When we look at life through the consciousness of our empowered soul, we can begin to live in a more gentle manner and respect all forms of life. This is one of the reasons that many people who are in touch with their soul turn to a vegetarian diet. They feel that God has provided enough food in the form of plants to sustain us and it is not necessary to take the life of animals, birds, or fish for food.

Buddhists, Jains, and Hindus alike, recognizing that the soul transmigrates and that sometimes it is human and other times it may inhabit another life form, will not take the life of any creature. In their view, there is a soul within every life form, and each soul has as much right to live as do human beings. They also recognize the law of karma, in which we have to account for all we do. If we take a life, one day we will have to pay for that act.

There is a wonderful story in the *Jataka Tales* of the Buddhists. In ancient times, some people followed the custom of offering a dead animal as a Feast to the Dead. One day, a teacher told his students, "I want you to bring me a goat to offer for the Feast of the Dead. Find a goat, take him to the river, and bathe him. When he is clean, place a garland of flowers around his neck." The students agreed and set off to find a goat. When they found one, they followed their teacher's instructions.

While they bathed and prepared the goat, the animal began to laugh, and the students were startled. Then the goat began to cry.

Thinking this to be very strange behavior, the students asked, "O, Goat, why did you laugh and then begin to cry?"

The goat replied, "Ask me this question again in front of your teacher." The students brought the goat to the teacher and explained the goat's behavior.

The teacher asked, "O, Goat, why did you laugh and then cry?"

The goat explained, "In one of my former lives I was a teacher like yourself. I also wanted to offer a Feast for the Dead, so I killed a goat. Because I killed that one goat, I had to be killed five hundred times by having my head cut off. This is my five hundredth and last birth. I laughed out of happiness, because today I shall be free from that one bad deed I had done."

The teacher asked, "Then what made you cry?"

The goat responded, "I cried when I thought that by killing me, you would have to be killed five hundred times in your future lives. I wept because I felt sorry for you."

The teacher, fearing the same fate might await him if he killed the goat, decided, "Do not fear, Goat. I will not kill you."

The goat said, "That doesn't matter. Whether you kill me or not, I am supposed to die today."

The teacher insisted, "Do not worry. I will protect you and see that nothing harms you."

The goat told him, "No amount of protection will help me. I cannot escape paying for my deeds of the past."

The teacher wanted to save the goat anyway, so he instructed his students to follow the goat around all day to make sure nothing hurt it.

Later that day, the goat became hungry. He told the students, "There is a bush growing near the top of that rock. I am going there to eat some leaves." As the goat ate the leaves, lightning flashed from the sky and struck the rock. A piece of the rock broke off and fell on the goat's neck. The goat was instantly killed.

When Lord Buddha was questioned by his own students about this story, he replied, "If you people only knew you would have to pay for your deeds, you would not kill any animals or living things anymore. You must pay for all your evil actions."

Some people are vegetarians because of their religious teachings, either because they believe in karma, a day of judgment, or they believe in the commandment, "Thou shalt not kill." Others maintain a vegetarian diet because they believe that animals have a right to live, or that they should not take a life if they cannot give back life. There have been many notable vegetarians throughout history. Early Greek philosophers such as Plato, Plotinus, Empedocles, Apollonius, Plutarch, and Porphyry followed vegetarian diets. Pythagoras instructed his followers not to defile their bodies by partaking of impure foods. He said that we have enough grains and trees which are loaded with fruits, delicious vegetables and roots that can be readily cooked, and no dearth of milk and honey. He told them that our earth has an abundance of pure, and harmless foods and there is no need for us to partake of meals for which blood has to be shed and innocent life sacrificed. Sir Isaac Newton, Ashoka the Great, Emperor Akbar, Percy Bysshe Shelley, Leo Tolstoy, Leonardo da Vinci, Albert Schweitzer, George Bernard Shaw, and Mahatma Gandhi were also noted vegetarians.

When we live life according to the guidance of the empowered soul, we find it difficult, if not impossible, to partake of the flesh of living creatures, because we see God's light in them. We begin to feel an affinity with our younger brothers and sisters, as did St. Francis of Assisi. Rabia Basri, the great Sufi saint, also experienced connectedness to all of God's creatures. Once, when she went into the mountains, she found herself surrounded by a group of wild animals. Deer, gazelle, mountain goats, and wild asses all approached her quietly. At that moment, Hasan-al-Basri arrived, but when the animals saw him, they fled in terror.

Annoyed, he asked Rabia, "Why did they run away from me in fear yet they were friendly with you?"

Rabia asked him a counterquestion, "What have you eaten today?"

He replied, "Some onion, fried in fat."

She pointed out, "You eat of their fat. Why should they not run from you?"

The empowered soul has respect and reverence for all forms of life. When we tap into the soul, our heart expands to invoke a connectedness with all living creatures.

##  Connectedness with Our Planet

Every year, millions of acres of rainforest are burned down. For the sake of converting the forest into more profitable farmland, people destroy life-giving trees. Trees are essential for oxygen production to maintain life on our planet. Through the process of photosynthesis, trees take in the carbon dioxide that we exhale and with the aid of water and sunlight, convert the ingredients to oxygen for us to breathe and into carbohydrates in the form of plant foods for us to eat. Yet one of the greatest suppliers of oxygen, the rainforests, are being destroyed.

The soul looks at everything from a broad view. It sees how human beings, plants, animals, the natural resources, and the earth cycles are all dependent on each other. The soul sees that in order for life to continue, we must be mindful of ecological issues. Polluted air and water mean potential diseases not only for our current population but also for future generations. Destroying the land will waste precious resources today and may deprive our children and grandchildren of what they need for a productive, comfortable life tomorrow.

When we connect with our soul, we are moved to make decisions regarding our planet's resources that benefit all humanity, current and future, and not just our own selfish ends. We are moved to take care of our personal part of the earth, and thereby help make global decisions to keep the planet safe from pollution and destruction.

##  Being One with Our Soul

When we talk about being connected with our soul, we are actually talking about self-realization. We are embodied souls—souls wearing a mind and a body. Thus, connecting with our soul involves a process of shifting our vision to see that we are not merely a mind and a body. When we identify with our soul, we empower it to guide our lives. We then think, speak, and act from the level of the soul.

Thinking, speaking, and acting from the central guiding power of our soul transforms our lives. How we look at the world and how we respond to it is no longer colored by the veil of our ego; rather, the vibrant living power of God in everything becomes crystal clear. The soul responds to people and nature as moving lights of God. It acts according to high principles of truth, nonviolence, purity, humility, love, and selfless service. It sees the interconnectedness of all living things, all people, and the planet.

Our soul puts us in touch with eternal wisdom, immortality, truth, peace, and love. As we live life through that perspective, we exist in a spirit of joy and bliss. We are fearless. We love everyone. We have access to divine wisdom and are in tune with our immortal nature.

## Being One with God

Being one with our soul leads to oneness with God. The soul is a drop of God and can merge with God. Think of a drop of water lying on a tabletop. If we pour a glass of water near it, the stream will pass the drop. The drop will automatically merge into the stream of water. It is still a drop, but it has become a part of the larger river. A raindrop falls into an ocean and becomes a part of the larger body. It still maintains its identity as a water droplet, but by becoming part of the ocean, it enjoys all the qualities of the ocean. So it is with our soul. When we identify with our soul, and the power of God draws us close, we merge into the ocean of God. We retain our identity, but we also have access to all that God is.

## ∞ **Activity** ∞

The following exercise is an analogy that can give us a sense of connectedness with all life. Picture a drop of water. Picture a stream flowing close by. The drop is pulled into the stream and merges into it. The stream enters the ocean as your soul connects with the ocean of life.

Saints, religious founders, and mystics have spoken of the merging of the soul with the eternal ocean. Because our language is inadequate to describe an experience beyond the intellect, these seers have resorted to analogies. Thus, a common motif is the image of the drop merging with the ocean or a ray of light merging with the sun. Where there were two, there is now only one.

In this regard, Christ has said:

*I and my Father are one.*

(John 10.30)

Shams-i-Tabrez, the Sufi saint, said:

*We have become so united, like body and soul, that hereafter no one can say I am different from Thee.*

In the Hindu tradition, in the Mandukya Upanishad, the state of oneness is described as follows:

*As the various mountain streams after passing through different plains fall into an ocean and lose their names and separate existence, so do the knowers of Brahman (God) merge in the illustrious, Self-Lustrous Being, losing their names and forms.*

The soul connected to God becomes indistinguishable from God. Duality disappears. Realization of the soul precedes union with God. We must first identify with the soul instead of with our mind and body. It is only when we can experience our soul that we can refocus our attention from the doorway of the world to the doorway of the spiritual regions. The soul can then travel through the spiritual regions to merge with God.

# Bliss

Another quality of the soul is unending, unfathomable, eternal bliss. The soul lives in a state of perpetual bliss. It is bursting with ecstasy that enraptures it day and night.

It is hard to describe the intensity of this bliss. The only analogy that we can give is to think of our happiest moments in this world and multiply them a thousandfold. For example, there are moments of great joy when we get married, give birth, receive a promotion, are recognized for our life's work, win a championship, save a life, or attain a goal. It may be difficult to imagine this, but the joys we may feel at these moments are but an inkling of the bliss we experience in the depths of our soul. If we can reconnect with our soul, never-ending rapture can stay with us throughout the day and armor us against the slings and arrows of life.

## Freedom from Pain and Sorrow

God has been described by saints and mystics as an ocean of love and bliss, free from pain and sorrow. The soul, being of the same essence as God, is also filled with love and bliss. In its primal essence, the soul is always enraptured and in ecstasy. Our soul in our original state is free from hatred, jealousies, pain, and suffering. There is nothing within the soul to cause sorrow.

It is hard for us as human beings to understand what this state could be like because we can find ourselves caught up in sorrow, pain, jealousy, hatred, and petty differences. If we reflect upon our lives, it may seem to us that we experience more moments of sorrow than joy. As Sant Darshan Singh once wrote in a verse about the human condition:

> *Even if a joy came my way,*
>   *it proved ephemeral,*
> *But every sorrow I received*
>   *seemed everlasting.*

We do experience times of happiness, but it seems that when we are faced with afflictions, they feel as if they could go on interminably. The question arises, If the soul is in bliss, why are we humans in pain or sorrow? Guru Nanak Dev, in talking of the human condition, said, "O Nanak, the whole world is full of sorrow."

When we empower our mind and body instead of our soul, we are far removed from the divine nectar of bliss awaiting us within. We are unaware of our true state of happiness. The reason that we are in pain and sorrow is that we are living at the level of the senses. It is like living in a dream state. Everything in the world seems real. Unless we awaken from the dream, our physical existence seems to be real. It is like we are Sleeping Beauty. Until Prince Charming comes and arouses her from sleep with a kiss, she remains unconscious. We, too, are sleeping. We need to wake up from this dream and experience the reality of our soul.

When we do so, we will then be in the state of perpetual bliss.

The supreme bliss can be reached when we stop identifying with the body, mind, and senses, and instead live at the level of the soul. We need to withdraw our attention from the outside world and focus it within in order to connect with the state of bliss. Then we can find ourselves free of pain and sorrow.

The state of bliss that the soul enjoys is beyond any experience in this world. Mystics and saints who have attained these blissful states have had to resort to metaphors and analogies to describe them. They have likened the inner ecstasy to marriage, the relationship between lover and beloved, love between a parent and child, the drinking of intoxicating nectar, drinking the water of life, absorption in celestial music, and visits to beautiful gardens with flowers, fountains, and pools. Each person experiences the bliss in his or her own way. Although the language used differs, the bliss is one and the same.

 **Intoxicating Nectar**

The description of the bliss as being analogous to the drinking of divine nectar appears in many religious traditions. The Sufis and Muslims speak of it as *Aab-i-hayat* or "Water of Life." The Hindus call it *Amrit* or the "Water of Immortality." The Christians also call it the "Water of Life." The Sikhs call it *Hari Ras* or "Divine Ambrosia."

In the *Gurbani* of the Sikhs, many references are made to *hari ras*. People drink wine or take drugs to reach a state of intoxication. But the saints and mystics do not need to drink wine or take drugs to get intoxicated; contact with their soul and God produces an intoxication that far surpasses any in this world. The Sikh scriptures say:

> *One who is awakened and made to drink this Ambrosia*
> *Alone knows the indescribable story.*
>
> (M 5 Gauri 13-16)

And:

> *Give up the love of the insipid water of evil,*
> *And drink in the divine Ambrosia of the Lord's Name.*
> *For because of not tasting it, myriads have been drowned,*
> *And one's soul is never in peace.*
>
> (M 5 Bilawal 802-819)

The intoxicants of this world are not lasting. Those who try to drown their sorrows in alcohol or drugs, do not find permanent bliss. They may find a temporary state in which they forget problems, but as the effects of the wine or drugs wear off, they are again faced with the same difficulties. Not only do they still face the same challenges, but often they have added to these problems because they now need money to buy drugs or alcohol, and their destructive behavior may have become harmful to their own health and safety as well as those of others. The intoxication one gets when one taps into the bliss of the soul, on the other hand, is permanent and lasting. It is safe. It does not harm anyone, and it is readily available, free of charge anytime one wishes to enjoy it. Guru Arjan Dev has said:

> *One is ever intoxicated,*
> *Who drinks the Ambrosia.*
> *Other drinks intoxicate,*
> *But their effect soon wears off.*
> *The God-intoxicated person drinks Ambrosia;*
> *For that one all other drinks become insipid.*
>
> (M 5 Asa 377-11)

And:

> *Pure is the Light and Soma Juice is the Word,*
> *A contact with them grants a selfless life of everlasting bliss.*
>
> (Ramkali M 5)

In the Bible, Christ says:

> *And let him that is athirst come, and whosoever will, let him*
> *take the Water of Life freely.*

(Revelation 22.7)

> *Whosoever drinketh of the water that I shall give him shall never*
> *thirst; but the water that I shall give him shall be in him a*
> *well of water springing up into everlasting life.*

(John 4.14)

Just as we need to drink water to quench our thirst, the soul's thirst is quenched by the love of God. That love flows like an eternal river from God, bathing all souls. The sleeping soul, however, remains unaware of its original state of bliss. The empowered soul is aware of that love and feels its wondrous ecstasy at all times.

 ## Bliss of Divine Union

Many of the mystics and saints refer to the bliss of the soul in terms of the happiness a bride and bridegroom feel on their wedding day. Images like lover and beloved, bride and bridegroom, bride and eternal spouse portray the relationship of the soul and God merging in a state of intoxicating love and bliss.

Mira Bai, a saint of India, considered herself wedded to the Lord. She wrote:

> *Perpetual are the nuptials of Mira Bai—*
> *Wedded as she is to the Eternal Bridegroom.*

And:

> *I have found everlasting fulfillment*
> *For I am wedded to the immortal Lord.*

In addition to using the image of bride and bridegroom at the time of the marriage, saints speak of the consummation of the marriage as an example of the bliss of the union between the soul and God. For example, St. Teresa of Avila, a Christian mystic, left behind numerous writings that give us insight into the bliss she experienced. In the *Interior Castle, 6th Abode*, chapter xi, she describes the bliss as "penetrating to the marrow of the bones, whilst earthly pleasures affect only the surface of the senses."

Kabir also talks about the ecstasy of union of the soul when it reunites with God:

> *When love struck and penetrated deep into my heart;*
> *Every pore of the body cried out, 'Oh! my Love. Oh! my*
>   *Love.'*
> *Without the help of lips to say that.*

In another verse, he says:

> *I have clasped the cup of Love to my heart,*
> *And it has permeated every pore of my body.*
> *Now I do not need any other medicine.*

Those who read such quotes may think the saints are speaking of a relationship between a lover and a worldly beloved, but they are actually trying to find a frame of reference for us to relate to the experience of the soul in communion with the Lord. Since the actual experience cannot be described in words, the analogy of lover and beloved can only give us a hint of what union with the Lord is like.

St. John of the Cross writes in his work *The Ascent to Mount Carmel*:

> *I continued in oblivion, lost,*
>   *my head was resting on my love.*
> *I fainted away, abandoned,*
>   *and amid the lilies forgotten*
>   *threw all my cares away.*[1]

The Christian German mystic, Meister Eckhart, wrote:

> Oh, wonder of wonders, when I think of the union the soul has
> with God! He makes the enraptured soul to flee out of
> herself, for she is no more satisfied with anything that can be
> named. The spring of Divine Love flows out of the soul and
> draws her out of herself into the unnamed Being, into her
> first source, which is God alone.[2]

##  Absorption in Celestial Music

Many mystics describe the bliss as being surrounded by a celestial
symphony whose music flows day and night. The empowered soul is
ever listening to enrapturing music, but it is not music of this world. It
is not made by any instruments or human voices. It is a melodious
sound that permeates the soul. This music emanates from God and
reverberates as an inner harmony within all souls. It is uplifting and
enrapturing. Like a siren's song, it keeps the soul ever captivated in its
blissful harmonies.

Scriptures of different religions are filled with references to this
inner music of the soul. Maulana Rumi says:

> Rise above thy mental horizon, O brave soul,
> And listen to the call of Music coming from above.[3]

Hafiz says:

> An unceasing Sound is floating down from the heaven,
> I wonder how ye are engaged in pursuits of no avail.[4]

Dadu Sahib says:

> The Eternal Music thundered in the heavens
> And I tasted the divine Nectar.[5]

Guru Arjan, the fifth Guru of the Sikhs, says:

> *Countless are the notes in the unending Melody,*
> *The charming sweetness whereof is ineffable indeed.*
>
> (*Sarang* M5 Naam, p. 183)

And:

> *The All-pervading Music is going on everywhere,*
> *In the heart of all, the Divine Music flows.*
>
> (*Vadhans* M5 Naam, p. 183)

Many people derive happiness from listening to the music of the world. People listen to the radio, buy audiotapes and compact discs, attend concerts, or create their own music. There are many sensations we may feel from outer music, such as joy, peace, excitement, or inspiration. But the music of the soul is an experience far beyond any we receive from listening to outer music. It is an enrapturing experience in which our soul is uplifted into spiritual realms. The bliss that fills the soul from listening to the inner musical vibration is many times greater than any worldly happiness. Once one listens to the music within, one wants to go on hearing it continually. Many who have listened to the music of the soul find that the outer music pales in comparison. They would much rather tune into the broadcast coming from their own soul than to any radio station in the outer world.

## 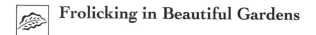 Frolicking in Beautiful Gardens

Another image of bliss that is used by mystics and saints is the pleasurable experience of strolling through a beautiful garden. Gardens are considered to be among the most beautiful places in the world. If anyone has been fortunate to visit a place like Kashmir in the foothills of the Himalayas, or the beautiful Swiss Alps, or other mountainous areas, one would understand the joy one feels at seeing the mountains, cascading waterfalls, forests, lakes, streams, and beautiful flower gardens. It is a rejuvenating and refreshing experience to bask in some of the most beautiful and scenic spots of nature. Yet the regions of the soul are far more blissful and breathtaking. The outer beauty of nature in this world is but a mere reflection of a more spectacular beauty within.

Soami Shiv Dayal Singh, an eighteenth-century saint from India, used this image frequently in his description of the inner bliss. He spoke of the gushing fountains, beautiful gardens, and pools of immortality in which the soul, depicted by the image of a *hansa*, or swan, enjoys wondrous delights. When he speaks of fountains, though, he refers not to rushing water, but to fountains of light, love, and bliss. There is no matter in the regions of the soul; but the analogy makes the image more recognizable to us. Comparing the bliss within to the joy of being in a delightful garden gives us but a taste of what awaits us.

 ## The Bliss Remains

Experiences of bliss are lasting. Their residual effects remain with us long afterward and sweeten our life. Their recollection often brings tears of joy to one's eyes and elation to one's heart. For example, St. Ignatius of Loyola confessed to Father Laynez that one hour of meditation at Manressa had taught him more truths about spiritual things than all the teachers combined could have taught him. One day he had an inner experience of the plan of divine wisdom in the creation of the world. On another day his soul was ravished in God. He was given insight into the mystery of the Holy Trinity. "This last vision flooded his heart with such sweetness, that the mere memory of it in after times made him shed abundant tears."[6]

Once we drink from the waters of immortality, we are filled with a ceaseless intoxication. Sant Darshan Singh has written volumes on this topic. He says: "What is the condition of such a soul as it returns to live out its lifetime in this world? How can it forget the ecstasy it has experienced, the joy, the peace, the intoxication which goes beyond human understanding?"[7]

Sant Kirpal Singh has said, "When that joy, that ecstasy is known, all other joys are forgotten."[8]

##  Bliss Makes One Oblivious to One's Pain

So powerful is the bliss of the soul, that one can actually undergo pain and sorrow in this world, and while feeling them, be able to sustain them in a state of bliss. This is quite paradoxical and hard to understand. The closest analogy we can have is that of certain medications that a doctor or a dentist may administer. You feel the pain but your mind is not bothered by it. The medication puts you in a state in which the pain is experienced in the body, but the message to the brain is blocked in such a way that you can bear it and be oblivious or unmindful of it. Although this is but a weak analogy, it gives some idea of the dual effect of both experiencing the pain of the world, while the bliss bathes you from within so that you can remain unaffected by it. As Kabir says:

> I have tried many medicines but found none more effective than love.
>
> When Love starts in one part of the body, it spreads and turns the whole body into gold.

St. Teresa of Avila has beautifully described this condition.

> Often, infirm and wrought upon with dreadful pains before the ecstasy, the soul emerges from it full of health and admirably disposed for action ... as if God had willed that the body itself, already obedient to the soul's desires, should share in

*the soul's happiness.... The soul after such a favor is animated with a degree of courage so great that if at that moment its body should be torn to pieces for the cause of God, it would feel nothing but the liveliest comfort.*[9]

This passage gives a glimpse into how one who has empowered the soul can face even torture. How else could Jesus have borne his crucifixion? Guru Arjan Dev, the fifth Guru of the Sikhs, was martyred. He was made to sit on a hot iron plate under which fire was burning, and red-hot sand was poured on his body. Burn blisters formed all over his body. A Muslim saint, Hazrat Mian Mir, could not bear to watch this and told Guru Arjan Dev that he was prepared to raze the entire Muslim empire to the ground in retaliation for what had been done to him. But Guru Arjan Dev refused the offer and replied, "Sweet is Thy will." What state of bliss the soul is in to withstand such torture and still have the love and trust in the Lord!

## ∞ **Activity** ∞

Think about the greatest bliss you have experienced in life. Relive the moment. Experience it through every pore of your being. Now picture that bliss multiplied a hundredfold. Imagine yourself experiencing that bliss even while undergoing painful moments in your life such as disease, injury, or loss. Make that bliss a part of you through all aspects of your life.

∞

When we empower the soul and drink of its blissful nectar, we still face life's pains and problems, but a current of intoxication supports us from within. It is like the arms of a mother supporting her infant while the child receives an injection from the doctor. The love of the mother enables the child to withstand the pinprick. It is also like the potter keeping his or her hand in the clay pot to hold the vessel's shape from within, while the machinery shapes it with force from without.

Sant Darshan Singh has written:

> *I pray that your intoxicating glances*
>   *Make me a stranger to pain and sorrow, O Cupbearer.*

This is the condition that can be ours when we empower our soul and identify with its state of perennial bliss.

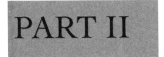

PART II

*Obstacles to Knowing Our Empowered Soul*

# Limited Vision

The soul bathes in a state of unlimited wisdom, immortality, unconditional love, fearlessness, connectedness, and bliss. Yet few of us are aware of its condition. We are aware of our physical body and our mind, but remain oblivious to our soul. We often limit our vision to the world outside. Most of our life is spent dealing with issues of worldly life, and few people spend time to peep into the inner world. The two worlds exist concurrently, but we have explored only one. Thus, we remain in ignorance of a territory more beautiful and fulfilling than we could ever imagine.

How could such an unlimited ocean of bliss and wisdom remain hidden from us? We are like fish swimming in the ocean, wondering where the water is. What is the reason for our limited vision?

##  How Do Our Body, Mind, and Senses Help the Soul Function in the World?

The root cause of our oblivion to our true state is due to the empowerment that we give our mind, body, and senses. When we enter human existence, the soul is provided with a physical body and a mind. These are necessary so that the soul can function on this physical earth. The soul is not made of matter. It is a conscious entity. It is spirit, made of the same essence as God. If we did not have a physical body we could not touch anything or interact with anything made of matter. We would not be able to move, hold, or manipulate any objects of this world. We would be invisible.

Without the body, we would not have a brain. The brain is like a computer that receives and interprets messages from the world to our mind and soul and sends messages back to the world. The brain is the controlling center for the five senses. Light falling on the eyes is sent through the optical nerve to the brain where the information is interpreted so that our mind knows what we see. Sound waves entering the ear are sent through the auditory channel to our brain so we can interpret the sounds and speech that we hear. The language area of our brain comprehends what we hear and generates a response. The brain picks up information from our sense of smell and taste as well. Receptors on our skin and throughout our body send messages to the brain about what we are feeling. Thus, we know when we have touched something hot or cold. These senses are ways for us to know where our soul is in the world of time and matter. It is also a way to communicate our thoughts, feelings, ideas, plans, and creations to the outer world. When we need something, the brain allows us to convey messages to others so we can have the food, water, oxygen, clothing, shelter, and protection from harm we need to keep our physical body alive.

If we did not have a mind, we would not be able to think about the information we receive from the world. The mind has many functions. It analyzes data, makes decisions and choices, has desires, makes plans, remembers, creates, and destroys. The mind is occupied by the information it receives from the world through the brain. The mind is easily caught up in worldly temptations. Thus, it is easily dragged out into the world through the senses.

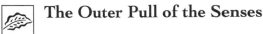 ## The Outer Pull of the Senses

The sense of sight is powerful and makes up a great part of our sense impressions. We are attracted to beautiful scenery, nice clothing, and fine paintings. We watch the activity of the world and are often caught up in its happenings.

Through the sense of hearing we are attracted to outer music, sounds of nature, and the conversations of others. A good portion of our day is spent talking and listening to others. We get involved in conversation at work, home, or at play. Our homes are filled with the sounds of radio, television, music, and computers with sound capability. There is so much to listen to and so much to learn. The mind is ever captivated by the chatter of this world.

The remaining sensory input comes from the senses of smell, taste, and touch. The mind is caught up in the fragrant smells of the earth: perfume, flowers, food, and nature. We know how attracted our mind is to the sense of taste. We seek out delicious foods to tantalize our taste buds. We go to different restaurants to enjoy new taste sensations. Advertisements entice us to try new flavors of food and drink. Much time is spent in the pursuit and enjoyment of delicious meals.

The soul, which is all-powerful, should be in control of our mind, and our mind should have control over the senses. But so powerful are the attractions of this world that our senses are drawn into them. The messages sent from the senses to the mind are so compelling that the mind becomes caught up in their never-ending panorama. Thus, our soul is helpless as the mind is occupied and preoccupied with the world. In the Chandogya Upanishads of the Hindus, it is said:

> *This body is mortal, always gripped by death, but within it dwells the immortal Self. This Self, when associated in our consciousness with the body, is subject to pleasure and pain; and so long as this association continues, freedom from pleasure and pain can no man find.*

> (Chandogya Upanishad 8.12.1)

The subtle spirit is lost in the heavy world of matter. Its faint callings go unheard as the mind competes and overpowers it with its whirlwind of worldly activity.

 ## Why Has the Soul Been Overpowered?

How could such a powerful soul be overpowered by the mind and the senses? The answer lies in that the outer expression of the soul is attention. Our attention is drawn by the mind and senses into the carnival of the world. Picture a child attending its first fair. The parents hold the child's hand as they lead him or her into the fair. But once there, the child demands to go on this ride and that one, to visit this booth and that one. The parents, wanting to make the child happy, find themselves led around from one attraction to another. Similarly, the attention finds itself being dragged around by the mind from one worldly pursuit to another. The result is that the mind takes control. Even if the soul wants to take back its power, the mind has created such a strong habit of focusing the attention on the world that is becomes difficult for the soul to regain control.

The mind's habits are strong. We all know how hard it is to break a habit. People who are in the habit of drinking or smoking find it difficult to stop the mind from engaging in these pursuits, even though it consciously knows these are harmful to the body. Some of us find that if we are in the habit of waking each day at a certain hour for work, on our day off we habitually wake up at the same time, even if we do not want to. There are numerous habits we find difficult to break. Similarly, the mind has been in the habit of directing our attention into the outer world.

If we could regain control of our attention and focus it within, we would then empower our soul. The empowered soul would then be the owner of the house. We would discover the hidden riches waiting to be uncovered.

## Our Attention is Habituated to Awareness of the World

Our vision is limited to the outer world of mind and matter. Since birth, we are taught to focus on the world's playthings. Who teaches us to go within? Can we recall our parents or teachers showing us how to expand our vision to our untapped side? Has anyone ever directed our attention within when we were growing up? If not, then our attention, led by the mind, was habituated to focusing its vision only on the outer world. Whatever our age, that is how long we have been in the habit of looking outside. The longer our attention has been focused on the outer world, the more entrenched we are in that habit.

Think about daily life. From the moment we wake up until the moment we retire at night, we are bombarded by the world. In the morning, those of us who have to work go through the routine of getting ready. We may have family obligations that need our attention. The newspaper, with its attention-getting headlines, calls for attention as well. Someone may turn on the television or radio to get the news, traffic, and weather report. Then, after getting dressed and eating breakfast, we are off to work. Our attention is focused on getting to work on time despite road construction and traffic delays. At work, while attending to our jobs, there are often conversations going on around us that pull our attention or distract us. After work, we battle the same traffic home. When we reach home, we may have chores to do or family responsibilities. We may find ourselves listening to summaries of what happened to our spouse or children during their day. Then the television comes on again and may run for several hours. By the time the rest of the family has gone to bed, we may be exhausted and ready for sleep. Day after day continues in a similar fashion. It seems there is no time for us to sit in the stillness of ourselves and discover who we really are. Unless we try to focus our attention within, we cannot know our soul and empower it to take charge of the attention.

## ∞ **Activity** ∞

Keep a journal of your day. Note where your attention is drawn and what sense is involved as you go through your daily activities. Calculate how much time you spend in the stillness of your self each day.

∞

 ## Expanding Our Vision

There is a story of two frogs who spent their whole life in a well. One day one of the frogs jumped out of the well and disappeared. He was gone for several days, and when he returned, the other frog asked him where he had been.

"There is such a whole big world out there beyond the well," said the first frog, and he began to describe all the sights and sounds he saw and heard.

"You must be making all this up," said the second frog. "There is nothing but this well. You are imagining all the things you have told me. If there were all those things you describe, then surely they would be here in the well. I have not seen them. They cannot possibly exist."

Often we are like that second frog. We may think that because we have not seen all there is to see, that nothing else exists. We may think this world is all there is to creation, instead of realizing the possibility that there is more than this physical universe. We close our mind like the frog in the well. With experimental mentality we would say, "Maybe there is more to life than what I see. Let me experiment for myself to find out if I am more than my body and mind."

There was a time when people believed the world was flat, until explorers proved the world was round. There was a time when scientists believed the earth was the center of the universe and the sun revolved around it, until they discovered this view of the universe was false. There was a time when we thought matter was solid, until we discovered that within the atom are many subatomic particles that, at their core, are dancing packets of energy. The findings of the last few centuries should tell us that what we formerly believed to be the nature of the world and our physical reality, may not be so at all.

Throughout the ages, there have been people with vision who discovered their soul. They left behind accounts of their experiences in the form of scriptures and oral traditions, which were then recorded by their students. We are their beneficiaries and we can try these techniques for ourselves. With some practice, we can expand our inner vision. We just need to learn the technique to do so.

We need a burning desire to find out who we really are. We need a yearning to know our true selves. We know that when we want something intensely, we can become so one-pointed that we can block out other distractions. When the desire to know our true self awakens, we can put our time and attention into finding it. All the other distractions begin to fall away. When we desire to awaken our soul, the soul responds, and its faint callings can be heard. Its own power starts to stir, and our attention can no longer ignore it. The stronger the cry, the more our attention is drawn to it. With time, the call of the world can become fainter and fainter as our attention is pulled irresistibly toward the love, the music, and the bliss of our soul.

# Aimlessly Adrift 9

Are we adrift in the sea of life, cast about from one turbulent problem and crisis to another? How can we fulfill the purpose of our life?

When we neglect to focus on our soul, time passes, and the goal of our precious human life is in danger of going unfulfilled. Most of the time we are so busy we hardly have a moment to think about our life, our goals, and our priorities. It seems at times that our life is not really our own. Our daily schedule is often controlled by our employer or family members who need us. The number of days we work, our holidays, and vacations are often fixed by our job or the amount of money we must earn. The body's needs also constrict us. We must eat a certain number of calories a day. To buy the food we need, we have to earn a living. We must work to pay the bills related to our living expenses. When we get sick, we need to spend time to cure the illness. If we have children, we need to attend to their schooling, their play, and their physical and emotional needs. It seems that there is hardly a spare moment left just to sit in stillness and reflect on where our life is going.

**How Do We Currently Spend Our Time?**

A number of studies have examined how much time we spend on different activities in our life. The results are surprising. For example, suppose our life span is seventy years. If we sleep eight hours a day, that means we spend twenty-three years of our life asleep. If we work forty hours a week from age twenty to age sixty-five, a total of forty-five years, that amounts to fifteen years of labor. If we spend two hours a day eating and preparing meals, that amounts to about six years. If we spend one hour a day dressing and undressing, plus time for washing, making, or buying clothes, that can average to about five years. It is possible that we could spend one year of our life talking on the telephone, three years waiting for people or standing in line, six years driving a vehicle, six years participating in leisure activities, and two years doing chores or other tasks. That leaves us three years. For those who go to a place of worship for two hours once a week, that leaves us with less than two years. Our time is so consumed by activity that only two years spread throughout our life are available for spiritual practice.

In the Sikh scriptures it is said:

> *In sleep our nights are wasted,*
> *In filling our belly the days:*
> *This life, precious as a jewel,*
> *Is forfeited for a cowry shell.*
> *Ignorant fool!*
> *You who have never realized God's Name,*
> *In the end into regrets shall fall.*
>
> (Adi Granth, Gauri Bairagani, M.1, p. 156)

It is easy for days to turn into weeks, weeks into months, months into years, and years into decades. Before we know it, much of our life has passed. Where did time fly? Where did it all go? What was it all about? Did we make the best use of our life? These are questions many ask at some time in their life.

##  Making the Best Use of One's Time

There is a story about a poor woodcutter who worked hard to earn his livelihood. One day, the king was passing through the woodcutter's part of the woods and saw the man working diligently. He felt sorry for the man's poverty and wanted to do something to help him.

"Woodcutter," said the king, "I have some land with sandalwood trees on it. I will give you the land so you can use it to become rich." The woodcutter thanked him and took over as the new owner of the land. He did not realize the value of the sandalwood trees so after cutting them down, he sold them for the same price as the regular trees. After the woodcutter had felled most of the trees, the king returned. Expecting to see the man rich, the king was shocked to find him still living in poverty.

"How is it that you have not made any money from selling the sandalwood trees?" inquired the king. "Those trees are worth a lot of money."

The woodcutter realized that he had lost a golden opportunity. There were but a few trees left. But he was able to sell those remaining ones for the correct value and earn enough to live on comfortably.

The story of the woodcutter is the story of our life. The sandalwood is equivalent to the number of breaths we are given in our lifetime. Like the woodcutter, we waste much of this precious breath and time on useless pursuits. Instead of amassing spiritual riches with our gift, we waste the time on petty pursuits. Time is precious. Once gone we can not retrieve it. Let us make the best use of our time. If we do so, then we can amass spiritual wealth far beyond our wildest dreams.

There is a saying that helps remind us about the importance of every breath. Think about each moment. For what do we trade away a moment of our life? Do we want to trade it away for thoughts of anger or greed? Do we want to trade it away to brood over the past or worry about the future? Do we want to spend it on pastimes that have no value for us? Or do we wish to spend the moment to discover who we really are and why we are here? What is the most valuable use of that moment for us in our life?

Let us not be aimlessly adrift on the sea of life. We need to spend some time to decide the direction in which we wish to go. Sant Kirpal Singh spent time in his early years deciding what he wanted to do with his life. After much soul-searching, he finally decided, "God first, and the world next." He decided that attaining self-knowledge and God-realization was his first priority. With that goal in mind, his course was set, and he did not stop until he reached it.

If we look at the life of great people, we find that many of them chose a direction in life. They may have pursued various interests—art, a hobby, science, research, or spiritual growth—but they all held one thing in common. They were not aimlessly adrift; they set a course and followed it.

Tegh Bahadur, the ninth Guru of the Sikhs, spent years meditating in a small room until he found God. Lord Buddha left his kingdom to go in search of enlightenment. He spent years seeking answers to questions about the nature of the world and our existence. Prophet Mohammed spent many years in a cave in pursuit of Allah.

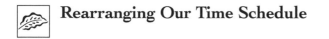 **Rearranging Our Time Schedule**

If we really wish to discover our soul, we need to allot time to achieve this. We have seen how easy our life can be eaten away by the simple task of keeping our physical body alive and healthy. Activities such as eating, sleeping, dressing, and working occupy a good portion of our time. With little time left over, we want to evaluate how to make the best use of it. Like the woodcutter, we do not want to throw away the precious gift of time.

Let us analyze our day in terms of twenty-four hours. Based on the calculation of time spent in our life span, we could divide our days as follows:

| | |
|---|---|
| Sleeping | 8 hours |
| Eating | 2 hours |
| Dressing | 1 hour |
| Travel | 2 hours |
| Work | 8 hours |
| Chores | $1^1/_2$ hours |
| Leisure | $1^1/_2$ hours |
| Total time: | 24 hours |

How can we fit in time for finding our soul? We may be able to subtract time from our sleep. Medical studies have shown that activities such as meditation or deep prayer produce feelings of rest and relaxation.

From where can the remaining time be taken? If our workday is fixed, the amount of time we spend eating, dressing, and doing chores is unchangeable, which leaves only the $1^1/_2$ hours of leisure time. Thus, it is possible for us to add more time to the two hours subtracted from sleep. Even if we devote two hours a day to our soul, that amounts to a total of six years throughout our life span. When we think about the amount of time we spend going to school or training for a career, that does not amount to a lot of time in the course of our life. If we truly wish to uncover the luminosity and riches of our soul, six years does not seem like a long time to devote to our spiritual quest. The more time we can devote to this quest, the better.

## ∽ **Activity** ∽

Make a time chart of your day. Plan a new chart in which you incorporate time for meditation. Try to make time for meditation a part of your daily routine.

∽

 ## **Setting Goals**

It is critical to set goals for ourselves. This is a good practice not only for our spiritual quest, but for all aspects of our life. If we wish to have a certain career, we need to devote time to study and learning. If we wish to amass a certain amount of money, we need to plan for our savings. If we wish to develop a hobby or talent, we need to put in practice time to become proficient. Similarly, if we wish to develop the spiritual side of our life and empower our soul, then we need to plan time for that goal as well.

Oftentimes, people make their spiritual pursuits their last priority. They do all the things they wish to do each day, and if there is time left over they may devote it to their soul. But all too often, we become so caught up in the storms of life that no time is left over for our soul. Thus, we may need to adjust our life so that we take time first for our soul. If we can first allot several hours a day for spiritual pursuits and keep that as sacred time for ourselves, and then fill up the other hours with the activities in our life, we can achieve our spiritual goal.

The key to making spiritual time a priority is to evaluate its importance in relation to the rest of the time we spend, mostly in the upkeep of our physical body. If we exist solely to maintain the physical body, then what do we gain? If we wish to achieve more than just the upkeep of our body, if we wish to develop our intellectual side, our cultural side, our spiritual side, or make a contribution to the world, then we must allot time for these pursuits.

If we devote time to the spiritual side and empower the soul, then we will find that growth in other aspects of our life comes easier. When we tap into our soul and its infinite wisdom, its bliss, its immortality, its fearlessness, and its connectedness, we find that we can more fully develop our other sides. It can help us improve our performance in many aspects of our life. It is similar to putting money in a savings account; the money will accrue interest that will help us with our other expenditures later on.

The choice is ours. If we wish to empower our soul and enjoy its gifts, then we can set priorities for our daily life and stick to them. We may find other creative ways to manage our time and devote it to empowering our soul. By doing so, we can enjoy inner bliss, peace, and love.

# Layers Covering the Soul

**10**

Our soul has many layers covering it. These layers are the impressions accumulated throughout our life. These impressions are imprinted on us from all our thoughts, words, and deeds. If our actions are negative, it is as if we add dark spots on a clear complexion. These dark spots must be removed before we can experience the luminous soul. The blemishes can be caused by thoughts, words, or deeds arising from anger, lust, greed, attachment, and ego, keeping us from experiencing the pure energy and power of the soul. We need to remove the coverings that block the luminosity of our soul.

To understand this, let us use the example of an electric light. The filament that radiates light is encased in a glass bulb, a thin covering clear enough so that the light can shine through. But if we put a lampshade around the bulb, the light is dimmed a bit. When we look at the lamp, we see light shining from the shade, but are not aware of the actual bulb. If we put a colored cloth over the lampshade, the light becomes even dimmer and takes on the color of the cloth. We become less aware of the brilliant white light emitted by the bulb. If we then put a sheet or blanket over the lampshade, the light is much dimmer. The more coverings we add, the less we see the light. It is the same with our soul. Our soul shines with a brilliance greater than many suns. What power and luminosity it has! But it is covered by many layers of anger, lust, greed, attachment, and ego.

##  Soul's True Nature Is Love

God is love. The soul is of the same essence as God. Thus, the soul is also love. Where there is love, there is no room for violence and anger. Where there is love, there is no room for dishonesty, deceit, and lies. Where there is love, there is no room for greed and selfishness. Where there is love, there is no room for ego. And where there is purity, there is no room for lust. If any negative quality takes possession of a relationship, love suffers. If negative qualities blemish our soul, we are distracted from our empowered state.

Let us think about the times in which we loved someone with all our heart and soul. It may have been the love between parent and child, best friends, spouses, or lover and beloved. When we love somebody, could we ever dream of hurting them in any way? Could we ever think of being dishonest and lying to them? Could we ever think of hurting that person to fulfill our own lust? Could we ever think of being selfish and greedy, of not sharing and giving them what they need?

The beautiful prayer of St. Francis of Assisi sums up the state of how the empowered soul deals with life:

> *Lord, make me an instrument of Thy peace;*
> *Where there is hatred, let me sow love;*
> *Where there is injury, pardon.*
> *Where there is doubt, faith;*

*Where there is despair, hope;*
*Where there is darkness, light;*
*And where there is sadness, joy.*
*O Divine Master, grant that I may not so much seek to be*
    *consoled as to console;*
*To be understood as to understand;*
*To be loved as to love;*
*For it is in giving that we receive;*
*It is in pardoning that we are pardoned;*
*And it is in dying that we are born to eternal life.*

The soul operates from a place of love. All its decisions are based on love. All its actions are moved by love. We can find out who is running our show by evaluating whether we are motivated by love or by anger, lust, greed, attachment, and ego. Whenever these five deadly passions raise their ugly heads, we can be sure the soul has been overpowered. As it is said in the Sikh scriptures:

*Five are the robbers lodged in this body—*
*Lust, wrath, avarice, attachment, and egoism.*
                      (Adi Granth, Sorath, M.3, p 600)

In the Christian scriptures, it is said:

*Now the works of the flesh are plain: fornication, impurity,*
*licentiousness, idolatry, sorcery, enmity, strife, jealousy, anger,*
*selfishness, dissension, party spirit, envy, drunkenness,*
*carousing, and the like. I warn you, as I warned you before,*
*that those who do such things shall not inherit the kingdom of*
*God. But the fruit of the Spirit is love, joy, peace, patience,*
*kindness, goodness, faithfulness, gentleness, self-control;*
*against such there is no law.*
                      (Galatians 5.19-23)

Whenever we take charge and resist the pull of negative qualities, we put our soul back in the driver's seat. We can choose to live a life governed by goodness.

 ## How Is the Mind the Root Cause of Placing Layers on the Soul?

When the mind is driven by its desires, it can overpower the subtle soul. One would think the soul, with its infinite power, could be strong and resistant, but the nature of the world is such that the mind is operating in its home territory. The situation is similar to two basketball teams in the play-offs. The team playing in its home city has the home-court advantage. The crowds are cheering for this team, which is comfortable in its own environment. Similarly, the mind is at home in the world. The soul is but a guest visiting temporarily. The mind has the advantage in this world of matter, whereas the soul is out of its element here.

The mind's desires lead it into an array of situations to get what it wants. It will stop at nothing in the pursuit of fulfilling its wants and needs. In the Hindu scripture, the Bhagavad Gita, Arjuna asks Lord Krishna, "What is the force that binds us to selfish deeds, O Krishna? What power moves us, even against our will, as if forcing us?"

Krishna responds, "It is selfish desire and anger, arising from the state of being known as passion; these are the appetites and evils which threaten a person in this life. Just as fire is covered by smoke and a mirror is obscured by dust, just as an embryo is enveloped deep within the womb, knowledge is hidden by selfish desire—hidden, Arjuna, by this unquenchable fire for self-satisfaction, the inveterate enemy of the wise. Selfish desire is found in the senses, mind, and intellect, misleading them and burying wisdom in delusion. Fight with all your strength, Arjuna! Controlling your senses, conquer your enemy, the destroyer of knowledge and realization." (Bhagavad Gita 3.36-41)

If the soul cries out to be heard, it is in the form of the faint whisperings of our conscience. It takes extreme fortitude of willpower and inner strength to listen to our conscience. How many times have we faced a situation in which we felt we were crossing the line between right and wrong? We know what determination and strength we need to obey the small voice of conscience.

As the mind runs amok in its home court, it gets embroiled in the five deadly passions: anger, lust, greed, attachment, and ego. Each time we succumb to the mind's desires, more layers block our brilliant soul.

## How Do Anger and Violence Create the Layers Covering Our Soul?

The soul's true nature is nonviolence; anger is foreign to it. Think of a mother with her helpless infant. The mother dotes on the child. She is so filled with love for the child that there is no place inside her for anger. The infant may grab hold of the mother's hair, beat the mother with his or her fists, and soil the mother's clothes. The mother is filled with such love for the child that she can tolerate his or her behavior with understanding and compassion. This is a close analogy of how our soul functions when it is empowered.

The soul watches the play of the world from a place of peace and contentment. It is in tune with God and, thus, anger and violence are not part of its consciousness. An African proverb says: "Whoever does evil against another does not remember the Lord." The soul, through the mind's activities, becomes aware of violence and anger in the world but is not pulled in to respond to it. It is like the sun that is unconcerned with the passing clouds that interfere with its rays shining on the earth. It just continues to emit its warm, life-giving rays, knowing that the clouds will pass. The soul sends out rays of peace and nonviolence. If we empower the soul in our lives, it will remain calm and harmonious in the face of evil and violence and continue to emit its rays without obstruction.

If the soul is nonviolent, then how is it that people in the world succumb to violence? Violence occurs when we turn a deaf ear to the love in our soul and, instead, tune into the radio station of our mind. Our mind wants its desires fulfilled. When it does not get its way, it becomes angry. It thrashes out at anybody or anything that prevents it from fulfilling its desires.

What kinds of desire does the mind crave? Some people desire material objects: money, luxuries, fine homes, fancy cars, and expensive jewelry. Other people desire fame and glory. Still others want power. There are countless desires and countless expressions of anger in this world.

Anger manifests itself in many ways. We may be angry in our thoughts. Other people may not know what we are thinking, but the vibration of anger radiates from us. There may be some nonverbal expressions of the anger: our body language, facial expressions, or tone of voice. Even if we control these outer cues, vibrations of anger escape and can be felt by other people. We think that our thoughts cannot hurt anyone, but in fact they do make an impression that forms another layer on our soul as well as hurts the person with whom we are interacting. In the end, anger hurts not so much the person to whom it is directed, but the sender. Like a boomerang, it circles back onto us and can harm us. This is a higher spiritual law that cannot be broken, changed, or modified.

Another way anger is manifested is through words. We may lash out at someone with our tongue and say hurtful things. We may criticize, slander, and backbite others.

We may think we are not being violent when we do not physically hurt anyone, but this is a misconception. Sometimes the wound from a tongue slashes deeper than one from a sword. A physical wound may heal, but a barbed comment may last a lifetime. It is hard to forget a harsh word that cuts to the root of our heart. There is a saying: "Put brain in gear before engaging tongue." Mahatma Gandhi's injunction—"Speak only what is true, kind and necessary"—can guide us to think before speaking, lest we injure someone with our words.

Anger can also erupt into physical violence. There is violence between individuals, and there is anger expressed violently on a grander scale when people of one religion go to war with those of another. What is the sense in all that killing? Both groups believe in God, but simply call God by a different name and worship the Lord through different rites and rituals. All people come from the same Creator. Yet in fits of anger, they are ready to kill in the name of the Lord. If we truly follow our religion, we would obey the teachings of the founders. In the Old Testament, it is said: "You shall not kill." (Exodus 20.13) In the New Testament, we find an account of Jesus and his teachings on nonviolence. Someone tried to seize Jesus and a companion of Jesus reacted with violence toward the attacker. Jesus told his defender: "Put your sword back into its place, for all who take the sword will perish by the sword" (Matthew 26.51-52).

Anger on its largest scale results in atrocities. In this twentieth century alone, humanity has witnessed wars in which millions of people were killed. Unchecked anger continues to leave a trail of destruction that is difficult to heal.

The New Testament says:

> What causes wars, and what causes fighting among you? Is it not your passions that are at war in your members? You desire and do not have; so you kill. And you covet and cannot obtain; so you fight and wage war. You do not have, because you do not ask. You ask and do not receive, because you ask wrongly, to spend it on your passions.
>
> (James 4.1-3)

A victim of someone else's anger has to bear the pain of the assault. Yet it is the one inflicting the violence who is hurt the most. The result of our deeds returns to the sender manifold. In Buddhism, we find this wise saying: "A person is born with an ax in his mouth. He whose speech is unwholesome cuts himself with his ax" (Sutta Nipata 657-60).

The by-product of evil is that it forms a layer on our soul, preventing us from experiencing our inner beauty, love, and riches. We have a hidden treasure chest in our backyard, but our negative actions bury it deeper and we cannot avail ourselves of its wealth. We lose in the end.

There are bound to be differences in the world. Between any two people there are differences in opinion, outlook, and approaches to life. But why do these differences need to escalate into anger, and from anger into violence? The person being attacked is not going to come around to the attacker's point of view. Rather, the victim will move further from agreement, and the day may come when the victim will retaliate. The oppressed often becomes the oppressor. No one gains from violence. Only when we maintain a nonviolent stance can we attain harmonious solutions. The ultimate deterrent to anger and violence is to discover one's true self. We need to dig deep with strength to uncover our soul.

##  Falsehood, Hypocrisy, and Deceit

Falsehood, hypocrisy, and deceit create another layer over the soul. The soul deals in truth; it knows no lie. But the desires of the mind cause us to become enmeshed in a web of deceit to get what we want.

When we want something that does not belong to us, we may resort to theft or cheating to get it. We try to steal from others what is not rightfully ours. We may try to cheat or trick others into giving us what we want. To do so, we must deceive and tell lies. Someone who wants material objects, wealth, or power may use deceit in order to wrest these from others. But what we think we are getting is never going to equal in worth what we are losing. We may get hold of someone's wealth or power for awhile, but in the end, we cannot take them with us beyond the grave. The measures of worth in the Beyond are love and truth.

What we gained for a transitory moment on earth will be but a passing flash in the eternity of time that awaits us in the Beyond.

In various religious traditions, we find the same message: untruthfulness leads to sorrow and pain. In the Jain scriptures, it is said:

> *These acts are included in stealing: prompting another to steal, receiving stolen goods, creating confusion to overcharge or underpay, using false weights and measures, and deceiving others with artificial or imitation goods.*
>
> (Akalanka, Tattvartharajavartika 7.27)

And:

> *Falsehood implies the making of a wrong statement by one who is overwhelmed by intense passions.*
>
> (Upasakadasanga Sutra)

In Judaism, we find:

> *No man should talk one way with his lips and think another way in his heart.*
>
> (Talmud, Baba Metzia 49)

And:

> *No man who practices deceit shall dwell in my house;*
> *No man who utters lies shall continue in my presence.*
>
> (Psalm 101.7)

In Sikhism, it is said:

> *Dishonesty in business or the uttering of lies causes inner sorrow.*
>
> (Adi Granth, Maru Solahe, M.3, p. 1062)

Some lies stem from people trying to act and pose and be something they are not. This could manifest in the form of deceit or hypocrisy. We deceive others into thinking we are greater or more powerful than we are. We put on a show. We are two-faced and hypocritical, showing one color to some people, and another to a different audience. In Islam, it is said in Hadith that "there are three characteristics of a hypocrite: when he speaks, he lies; when he makes a promise, he acts treacherously; and when he is trusted, he betrays."

In the end, such acting and posing is discovered. The face of truth cannot be hidden for long. The punishment for deceit is very hard, because when others discover our sham, we are seen for our true nature. Those to whom we looked for approval turn against us and we have nowhere to hide. Most religious traditions warn against lying. In Buddhism, it is said: "A liar lies to himself as well as to the gods. Lying is the origin of all evils; it leads to rebirth in the miserable planes of existence, to breach of the pure precepts, and to corruption of the body" (Boddhisatva Surata's Discourse in Maharatnakuta Sutra 27).

In the Old Testament, it is written:

*Woe to those who call evil good and good evil,*
*who put darkness for light and light for darkness,*
*who put bitter for sweet and sweet for bitter!*

(Isaiah 5.20)

In the Qur'an, it is said: "Whoever commits a delinquency or crime, then throws the blame upon the innocent, has burdened himself with falsehood and a flagrant crime" (4.112).

The soul is Truth personified. It has nothing to hide and no need to lie. It is comfortable with who and what it is and needs not act and pose as something else. It is all-powerful so it needs no power from others. It is all bliss, so it needs no material objects for its pleasure. It is all love, so it need not try to own anyone else. It is one with God, so there is no need to be something other than what it is. When we empower our soul, the virtue of truth embellishes us. We need not act from a place of deceit, lies, hypocrisy, or falsehood. We can feel comfortable in the truth and need fear no one. In discovering our soul, our every thought, word, and deed is motivated by truth.

## What Role Does Greed Play in Forming Layers Around Our Soul?

Another way we add layers to our soul is through greed. The mind's desires have a leading role in this area. The mind is on a mad pursuit to fulfill its desires, and there is no end to what it wants because it is never satisfied. Its dissatisfaction takes two forms: it wants more and more of what it has or it tires of what it has and wants something else. Thus, the mind leads us on a never-ending chase from one thing to another. It is like running after a desert mirage. An oasis appears to be within reach, but when we near it, the oasis moves farther away. We keep chasing it, hoping to reach it, but its waters seem to continually elude us. So it is with happiness stemming from things of this world. The mind's thirst for attainment is never quenched. It becomes greedy for more. It thinks having more of what it already has will satisfy it, and the pursuit continues. It thinks it will be happy with what someone else has, and so it begins to covet from others. Or, it may find that what it obtains does not bring it the fulfillment it seeks, so it moves on to desire something else.

Greed leads us down many dangerous pathways. It keeps our attention diverted from our soul and God. It can lead to aggression and violence when we wish to take from someone else what is not ours. In the Taoist tradition, it is said:

> *There is no crime greater than having too many desires;*
> *There is no disaster greater than not being content;*
> *There is no misfortune greater than being covetous.*
>
> (Taoism, Tao Te Ching 46)

In order to satisfy our greed, we may lie to get what we want. Finally, greed can lead to selfishness. Rather than giving and sharing, we amass everything for our self. In the Jain scriptures, it is said:

> *The ignorant craves for a life of luxury and repeatedly hankers*
> *after pleasures. Haunted by his own desires he gets benumbed*
> *and is rewarded only with suffering.*
>
> *The benighted one is incompetent to assuage sufferings,*
> *because he is attached to desires and is lecherous. Oppressed by*
> *physical and mental pain, he keeps rotating in a whirlpool of*
> *agony. I say so.*
>
> (Acarangasutra 2.60, 74)

In the New Testament, it is written: "The love of money is the root of all evils" (Timothy 6.10).

Greed is the antithesis to the soul's innate nature, which is self-lessness. The soul wants to share all that is good with all creation. It is giving, loving, and caring. Whatever is good, it would not want to keep to itself, but would want everyone else to partake of it.

The soul is also content with what it has. Why shouldn't it be? After all, its true nature is to be one with God. Thus, it is complete in itself. It lives in an eternal state of bliss and happiness. It is not enticed by the transitory toys of this world, which are perishable. The sources of its happiness—God, the ocean of bliss, consciousness, and love—are forever.

When we identify with our soul, we are free of the impediments brought by greed. We can be content and enjoy the inner nectar and its bliss-giving waters. We need not covet what someone else has. We do not have to resort to violence or deceit to get what we need. The outer pleasures are insipid when we find inner fulfillment.

Greed clouds our pristine soul. If we could control our mind and empower our soul, then the seemingly endless cycle of chasing our desires could come to an end. We could be satisfied and content with our destiny. We could remain in a state of calm and view all that comes to us from God with serene acceptance. In this way, the fire of greed that consumes us could be extinguished.

When we empower our soul, we no longer burn with desire. We no longer waste precious moments seeking that which is perishable. Rather, we are satisfied and fulfilled from being in tune with that which is imperishable and permanent, our inner spiritual treasures.

In the Sikh scriptures, it is said:

> *What is that love which is based on greed?*
> *When there is greed, the love is false.*
>                    (Adi Granth, Shalok, Farid, p. 1378)

Sant Kirpal Singh used to say, "Love knows only to give, give, and give." When we are filled with greed, we know only to take, take, and take. When we open our heart to the voice of the soul, we open our hands to share with others. When we open our hands to share with others, we open the door to God.

##  How Lust for Worldly Pleasures Creates Blockages

Lust constitutes one form of desire—desire of the flesh. We tend to think of lust as only sexual gratification, but there are many expressions of lust, among them lust of the senses—of sight, sound, smell, taste, and touch. Each of our senses has a dual function: as a conveyer of information and data about the outside world to our brain, and as a means to experience the pleasures of the world. If we seek excessive gratification of the senses, if we seek excessive pleasure, then we enter the realm of lust.

Our eyes help us move around in the world, find objects we need, and avoid danger. They also are beholders of beauty. They are drawn to beauty in the form of fine art, magnificent nature, and attractive faces. But if we become obsessed with viewing these objects to the exclusion of our soul, our interest enters the domain of lust. We may notice that someone is beautiful, but when we are obsessed with looking at him or her with intent to take physical advantage of that person, then our interest enters the realm of lust.

Our ears help us communicate, learn, and alert us to possible danger. We also use them to appreciate fine music, the sounds of nature, or the voice of a singer. But when we become preoccupied with listening to impure talk, foul language, or discussions of sensual pleasures at the expense of time spent listening to the song of the soul, then we may enter the domain of lust. If the talk flares up desires, then it takes us far away from our soul.

Our sense of taste also has a practical function: to keep us from eating spoiled or poisoned foods. On the other hand, our taste buds help us appreciate a well-prepared meal made with care and love. But when we find that our appetite for foods becomes obsessive, then we enter the domain of lust. People can crave certain foods to a degree that their attention is diverted from the taste of the nectar provided within by the bliss and love of our soul.

We can also have lust for fragrance and smells. The sense of smell is a protective device that can signal the presence of smoke or the danger of fire. With the sense of smell we may also appreciate the fine fragrances that come from flowers or perfumes. When we become obsessed with this pleasurable side, to the extent that it takes our attention from the sweet fragrance in our soul, then the sense of smell enters the arena of lust. When a fragrance inflames our sensual passions, it leads us into the domain of lust.

The sense of touch is another tool to convey information about our surroundings. It tells us what is soft and comfortable and what is jagged and dangerous. It warns us about extreme hot or cold temperatures so we can protect our body. The sense of touch also allows us to appreciate the pleasurable sensations of smooth silk, soft cotton, or cool water. Touch enters the arena of lust, however, when we become obsessed with experiencing more and more physical sensations to the exclusion of experiencing the warmth of divine love within us.

Lust for pleasures of any of the senses can lead to addiction when a person loses the ability to control and monitor the desire to experience a pleasurable sensation. Thus, lust of the sense of taste may appear in the form of food or alcohol addictions. We may develop an addiction to the pleasurable sensations we experience internally or mentally from substances such as drugs.

With regard to the excess of desires, we find it written in Buddhist teachings that "the man who gathers flowers (of sensual pleasure), whose mind is distracted and who is insatiate in desires, the Destroyer brings under his sway" (Dhammapada 48).

The Christian New Testament says:

> *Let no one say when he is tempted, "I am tempted by God"; for God cannot be tempted with evil and he himself tempts no one; but each person is tempted when he is lured and enticed by his own desire. Then desire when it has conceived gives birth to sin; and sin when it is full-grown brings forth death.*
>
> (James 1.13-15)

And:

> *Do not get drunk with wine, for that is debaucher; but be filled with the Spirit.*
>
> (Ephesians 5.18)

In the Old Testament, it is written:

> *Woe to those who rise early in the morning, that they may run after strong drink, who tarry late into the evening till wine inflames them! They have lyre and harp, timbrel and flute and wine at their feasts, but they do not regard the deeds of the Lord, or see the work of his hands.*
>
> (Isaiah 5. 11-12)

When we do not experience the fulfillment of the soul, we seek satisfaction in the outer world. These outer pursuits may be a symptom that we are craving contact with God. We are longing for our original sate of bliss which, through attachment to and desires for things of this world, we have lost. Addictions are a sign of humanity's search for God. They represent a spiritual hunger that has been misdirected. Addictions can be resolved when we get in touch with God. If we are afflicted with lust, then we can overcome it by directing our attention to the place where we can find true fulfillment, within our own soul.

Our soul is free of lust. It does not need to crave the desires of the flesh because it is in perpetual union with the Lord. Its entire being is permeated with love and bliss. Any pleasures of this world appear to be tasteless in comparison with the divine taste of the Lord's nectar of love within. When we empower our soul, we no longer need the transitory pleasures of the world.

## How Does Attachment Form Layers Over Our Soul?

Attachment blocks our soul. Attachment is a quality of the mind; non-attachment is a quality of the soul. Lord Buddha instructed that one should "be desireless." Attachment brings us pain and sorrow. Why? When we are attached to something, we fear losing it. This fear sets off a chain reaction leading to negative behaviors. When we are attached to something we become angry when it is taken away from us. When we are attached to something that is not ours, we may lie and deceive to hold on to it. When we are attached, we may become greedy for more than we have. When we are attached, we may become obsessive and lustful. When we are attached, we may become selfish and reluctant to share. Attachment leads us to fall into a dark pit, from which there is a slim chance of escaping.

If we look at animals and insects, we see how even the attachment of one sense can lead to self-destruction. For example, the bee's attachment to taste causes it to land in the heart of a fragrant flower, which may close in on it and take its life. The moth's attraction to light causes it to fly into the burning flame and be consumed. In the Sikh scriptures, it is said:

> For love of the lotus is the humming-bee destroyed,
> Finding not the way of escape.
> Subdued by lust is the elephant caught,
> Helpless under others' power.
> For the love of sound the deer bows his head,
> Thereby torn to pieces.
>
> (Adi Granth, Dhanasari, M.5, pp. 670-71)

If one sense can overpower an animal, what about human beings who have been given five senses! Our human lives are flooded with sensory impressions from the world, to which we become attached.

Attachment can be a fatal blockage to experiencing our soul. We can be so attached to something that all our attention is focused on it, and we never bother to find our soul. If we lose that to which we are attached, the pain may be so great that we cannot concentrate on finding our soul. Or we may become so intent upon regaining what we lost, we seek fulfillment in the outer transitory world and never stop to look for the permanent happiness awaiting us within. Finally, we may become so obsessed with getting what we want, that we will stop at nothing to get it, even if it means being violent, stealing, cheating, deceiving, or lying. In this way, attachment keeps our mind empowered, rather than our soul.

The soul's true condition is detachment. Detachment, in this sense, does not mean disinterest or apathy. Rather, detachment means that we live in the world like a swan lives in water. It can swim in the water, yet fly with dry wings. We live out our life making the best use of what we need to keep our body alive, to earn our livelihood, to make a contribution to society, and to fulfill our responsibilities to our family and community, but we are not attached. We are able to accept what comes to us and also accept what is taken from us. We live in a manner in which we know that everything that exists comes from God and, as such, it is the property of God. Whatever is ours is given to us as a gift on loan. When the time for our loan is finished, we relinquish what we have with thanks for the time we had it, and not curse our fate. We take what comes to us with a spirit of acceptance and gratitude. This is the condition in which our soul lives. When a friend of Rabia Basri came to her with a bandage on his head complaining of the pain, she inquired, "How long have you had the headache?" The friend said, "A few hours." She then asked him, "For how long have you been without a headache?" He replied, "Many years." Rabia said, "For several hours you are wearing the bandage of complaint; yet for all those years you did not have a headache, you did not wear the bandage of gratitude." She impressed upon him the need to live in a state of acceptance of whatever God sends us.

When our soul is empowered, we remain unattached. If we can live in a manner in which we are not attached to anything transitory in this world, then we are truly free. We are free from the fear of loss and can enjoy the nonmaterial gifts that await us within.

## How Do Ego and Vanity Create Layers Around Our Soul?

It is said that of all the blockages to the soul, the last to be removed is the ego. Ego is both blatant and subtle. It causes us to forget our true self and God. As it is said in the Hindu scriptures:

> *Shun all pride and jealousy. Give up all idea of "me and mine."... As long as there is consciousness of diversity and not of unity in the Self, a man ignorantly thinks of himself as a*

*separate being, as the "doer" of actions and the "experiencer" of effects. He remains subject to birth and death, knows happiness and misery, is bound by his own deeds, good or bad.*

(Srimad Bhagavatam 11.4)

In the Buddhist tradition, it is said:

*Traveling powerless, like a bucket traveling in a well:*
*First with the thought "I," misconceiving the self,*
*Then, arising attachment to things with the thought "mine."*

(Candrakirti, Madhyamakavatara 3)

Rooting out the ego takes understanding and a firm grip on the mind. We may suffer from the ego of wealth in which we are proud of how much money we have or our expensive possessions. The ego may cause us to look down upon those who do not have as much as we have. Ego may even lead us to hurt the feelings of those who are not financially endowed.

We may have ego of knowledge in which we become proud of how much we know. We are full of vanity over the number of educational degrees we have. We may think we know more than anyone else at our job. We lack humility and think that we are the source of all knowledge and look down on others who know less than we do. Little do we realize that the source of all wisdom is within everyone. When we think we are more intelligent and knowledgeable than others, we may hurt those who are simpler in their thinking or who lack the amount of training we have.

There is also the ego of beauty. We may think we are the most beautiful of creatures. We may flaunt our looks to such a degree that we make others who are not as beautiful feel inferior. We may use our looks to assume power over others or to entice others into doing what we want them to do. We may act and pose and try to charm others into giving us what we want. This type of ego leads to a form of deception and hypocrisy. Through our looks, we may give the appearance of being something we are not. This may cause harm to others, but most especially harm to ourselves.

We can become an egotist when we talk too much about ourselves or think too much of ourselves. If our attention is on our outer being, our personality, looks, mind, or possessions, then we are certainly not going to be focusing on our soul. The soul is the source of all beauty, wisdom, and wealth, but we remain bereft of these gifts as long as we are filled with thoughts of our body and mind. The outer gifts will leave us one day and we will go empty-handed from this world. The Bible says, "Lay not up for yourselves treasures upon earth, where moth and rust doth corrupt, and where thieves break through and steal. But lay up for yourselves treasures in heaven, where neither moth nor rust doth corrupt, and where thieves do not break through and steal. For where your treasure is, there will your heart be also" (Matthew 6:19-21). Outer beauty fades with age. If we do not have beauty of spirit, few will be attracted to our outer beauty as wrinkles appear on our face. Knowledge is also temporary, for it changes every year. What we learned in elementary school may be obsolete today. The findings of scientists today will be outdated tomorrow. Knowledge is not a permanent foundation upon which to place our ego. Wealth can disappear with changes in the economy. Stocks and bonds may lose value, or a serious illness may drain our finances. There is no stability in wealth, which means that pride based on wealth stands on flimsy ground.

Our soul is free of ego. Thus, it is free from fear of the vicissitudes of life. Empowering our soul means we free ourselves from reliance on outer sources of pride to make us happy. Rather, we live in a state of eternal happiness with the state of our soul, because it is one with the Lord.

Ego takes many forms. It is said that among the ascetics and monks, the last enemy they must conquer is ego. They may give up desire for material possessions, they may give up lust, anger, greed, and attachment. But if they pride themselves on giving up these things, they are still subtly caught in the net of ego. That is how ego imperceptibly rears its ugly head.

It is said by the mystics, "Where I am, God is not. Where God is, I am not." In the Sikh scriptures it is written:

> *Where egoism exists, Thou are not experienced,*
> *Where Thou art, is not egoism.*
> *You who are learned, expound in your mind*
> *This inexpressible proposition.*
>
> (Adi Granth, Maru-ki-Var, M.1, p. 1092)

If God and the soul are one, there is no question of I and Thou. Both are Thou. In a story from the Sufi tradition, a man went to the door of God's house and knocked. God asked, "Who is there?" The man answered, "It is I." The door did not open for him. The man returned home without seeing God. He pondered for a long time about why God did not let him in and prayed for an answer. Finally, he had a moment of enlightenment; he knew what the problem was. He returned to God's house and again knocked on the door. This time when God asked "Who is there?" the man replied, "It is Thou." The door opened, and he attained communion with the Lord.

When we eliminate ego—I-ness, as it is called—we are then one with God and there is no separation between the soul and God. Sant Kirpal Singh used to say that God plus mind is man (the term *man* in his day encompassed all human beings); man minus mind is God. It is the ego that creates the illusion that we are separate from God. It is ego that creates the blockage that keeps us from empowering our soul.

##  How Do the Layers Create Forgetfulness of Who We Are?

Layers created by anger, lust, greed, attachment, deceit, and ego cause us to forget our true nature as soul. We have forgotten that we are love, truth, peace, bliss, humility, purity, nonviolence, and selflessness. We have forgotten God and have forgotten who we are as soul. It is said in the Muslim scriptures, "Be not like those who forgot God, therefore He made them forget their own souls" (Qur'an 59.19).

When we identify with our mind and senses, we continue to add layers over our brilliant soul through our immersion in the negative qualities and passions. Thus, our life becomes a continuous drama of pain and sorrow.

 ## How Can We Remove the Layers?

We need to remove the veils blocking our soul so we can shine with our own innate light. We need to unravel the cloths covering the lightbulb, so that there will be no veil left and we can exist in all our pristine glory. Saints and mystics spent their lives removing their coverings. Once they reached their core, they realized bliss, joy, and peace as their true nature. Wanting to share that with others, they taught humanity how to remove the coverings. They were each in touch with God's laws, and tried to convey this to the people of their times. They tried to impress upon their followers that the layers of anger, lust, greed, deceit, attachment, and ego are the mind's follies. They wanted us to know that the soul lives by the law of God—the law of love and truth.

A mammoth job lies in front of us. There are so many layers to uncover to reach our truth, but the task is possible. If we start now, we will get to the bottom of who we are. By following the teachings of the saints, mystics, and spiritual teachers, we will discover an instruction manual for removing the coverings that keep us from our soul and God.

 **PART III** *How to Access the Unlimited Energy of Our Soul*

# Meditation: Doorway to the Soul   11

The treasures of our soul remain hidden under layers of mind, matter, and illusion. Our attention is focused on the outer world instead of the inner one. We keep adding more coverings through our mind's desires, which lead us into anger and violence, lust, greed and attachment, deceit, and ego.

Is there any way to cut through these blockages to experience the soul? How can we not be washed away by the sea of life? Fortunately, saints and mystics throughout the ages have been able to venture into the realm of the soul. Just as pioneers explored the oceans when people believed the world was flat, and brave astronauts ventured into outer space, there have been explorers of the inner worlds of the soul. They overcame great obstacles, the pull of the mind and senses, to invert their attention within themselves. Discovering the doorway to the soul, they were able to enter it and remove the layers covering the soul so their true self could shine in all its pristine glory. They learned to structure their lives to find the time to live as an empowered soul. They learned how to balance their life to attend to their spiritual side as well as their worldly responsibilities. They learned how to drink of the spiritual nectar within as well as share their overflowing cup with those who were thirsty.

These inner explorers came from all backgrounds, all cultures, all religions, and all ages. Yet, they discovered the same way within and the same treasure. What they found was one and the same, but they used different terminology to describe it. The following chapters provide us with the roadmap they left behind so that we, too, can take the same journey. By studying how they realized their soul, we have an opportunity to reach our Creator.

##  How Can We Find the Soul?

Where is the soul in the body? What is its size and shape? Where do we look to find it? When we talk about the soul, we speak of its characteristics. But is there any physical way to describe our soul?

Our soul transcends physical description because it is not made of matter. Matter has weight and takes up space. But the soul is spirit and as such is not made of matter. As spirit, it is invisible. It is consciousness. When doctors dissect a body they find only matter. They cannot find the soul. The soul belongs to a dimension in which there is only Light and Sound, but not the light and sound we know of in this world. They are a much higher light and sound, of which the light and sound in the physical universe are but a reflection. We, as soul, are a light brighter than sixteen outer suns, yet it is not a scorching, burning light. It is a light that is soothing and loving. We vibrate with a celestial harmony that cannot be heard with our physical ears.

The soul is connected to the physical body through a silver cord that is invisible to the eyes. Saints and mystics have referred to this cord. It is a luminous thread or cord that allows the soul to transcend the body and travel into spiritual realms and return. At death, the silver cord severs from the body so that the soul does not return to the body. When the soul leaves the body in meditation, however, the silver cord remains intact so that the soul can return to the body.

The outer expression of our soul is attention. Attention is spread throughout our body. It is the soul that gives life to our body. A body devoid of a soul, or in which the silver cord has been cut, is not alive. The seat of the soul lies at a point between and behind the two eyebrows, in a place known as the third or single eye. It is also referred to as the tenth door, sixth *chakra*, *ajna chakra*, *daswan dwar*, *tisra til*, and mount of transfiguration. By concentrating on this point, we can gain access to the soul. This point is a doorway through which the soul can enter into the spiritual realms within.

## Where Are the Inner Realms?

When we completely focus our attention on the third or single eye, we find inner realms. These are inner dimensions that exist concurrently with our physical universe. For lack of better terminology, we speak of inner and outer, or higher and lower regions. These realms are states of consciousness that do not exist in time and space; only our physical world is measured in terms of time and space. The physical region, including the earth, sun, planets, and galaxies, exist simultaneously with the spiritual regions. We refer to the frame of reference as time and space because that is a measurement used in this physical universe. But all these regions, physical to spiritual, exist as states of consciousness. When we talk about traveling to the inner or higher regions, we are not actually traveling anywhere. We are actually refocusing our attention to a different state of consciousness or awareness. For example, let us recall a time when we were sitting and listening to a conversation. Suddenly, we remember something else that happened to us before and the whole scene, occurring at a different time and place, replays before our eyes. We have not gone anywhere but our location seems to have shifted in our mind's eye. Although traveling to an inner region is not the same as a daydream or figment of the imagination, there is a similar shift in consciousness in which we become aware of an inner region. Our physical body remains seated with closed eyes, but our soul becomes conscious of a different region or place.

An anecdote from the life of the Sufi saint Bulled Shah illustrates where we find the inner regions. Bulled Shah went to his teacher, Inayat Shah, for instruction on how to find God. Inayat Shah used the example of gardening to answer his student. He said, "Just as you transfer a plant from one side of the garden to another, transplant your attention from here to there." To find the inner realms, we need merely to shift our attention from the physical world to the spiritual realms. Instead of thinking about the world and our body, we focus our attention at a specific point, at the third or single eye.

In the Bible it is written, "The light of the body is the eye, if therefore thine eye be single, thy whole body shall be full of light" (Matthew 6:22). The light here is not intellectual wisdom; it is an actual light that one sees between and behind the two eyebrows. If our attention is concentrated at this single point, we can see the effulgent light of God.

Instructions for finding this center are often part of a secret oral tradition of the saints and mystics. The methods are not generally known to the masses, except to those who explore deeper into their religions and faiths to uncover the more mystic, esoteric side. As esoteric practices were handed down from masters to disciples through an oral tradition, little was written down. Fortunately, we find references in some scriptures, but most people, when they read these, gloss over them without realizing that they refer to a gateway into the Beyond. One who has gained access to this entrance understands the meaning of the references and can explain them to us. Then, once we ourselves grasp what the references represent, we realize that the scriptures are providing us with a roadmap to the same doorway.

##  How to Reach the Doorway

Knowing that there is a doorway into the Beyond located at the third or single eye is the first step. But how do we get to that doorway? How do we find that point? Saints and mystics throughout the ages have taught that the path to that doorway is through meditation. We need to withdraw our attention from the outer world and focus it at the center, leading to the inner realms. We must take our attention from without and focus it within.

## Focusing Our Attention

Our attention is the outer expression of the soul. Through the mind and senses, our attention is diverted to the outer world. We become engaged in what is happening outside of us through the information we receive from our senses. We are also occupied with the thoughts that run through our mind, most of which revolve around what has happened in the past or what will happen in the future. We mull over our problems from the past and we plan what to do in the future. Our thoughts are like running commentaries of what is happening. Our mind replays everything that happens, and processes it with comments on every play. We judge, analyze, criticize, and evaluate everything we take in. Thus, our mind is occupied continually with this world, and our attention is diverted from the right doorway into the Beyond.

We are similar to a blind man who is put in a room and told to feel his way around the walls for the doorknob to get out of the room. He goes on touching the walls, searching for the knob, but each time he nears it, he has an itch. He takes his hand away from the wall to scratch it, and thus misses the knob. Similarly, often when we get close to that doorway, a thought intervenes to distract us and keeps us from discovering the entrance. Left to chance, we, too, might not find the entrance. Therefore, we must consciously learn a technique to reach that point. Meditation is the method by which we can focus our attention at the third eye to find the doorway within.

 ## What Are the Light and Sound of God?

The beginning of our soul's journey is the contact with the Light and Sound of God. The Light and Sound are the two primary manifestations of God. It is said that when God desired to bring about creation, a current emanated from God. That current manifested as Light and Sound. It was a divine stream that brought all creation into being. As it moved further from the source, the vibratory rate changed. Thus, different regions of different vibrations were brought into being. The Light and Sound principle ultimately brought the physical universe into being.

Our physical universe is operating at the densest vibratory rate. It is so dense that it manifests as matter. It is only in the last few decades that scientists have begun to understand that what we thought was solid matter is really dancing packets of energy. At the core of matter is an energy that is light and sound. When we split an atom, there is a tremendous burst of light and sound. This light and sound energy within our physical universe is the densest vibration of the current of Light and Sound emanating from the Creator. It brought all creation into being and sustains all creation.

The Light and Sound current flows out from God, but it also flows back to God. We can catch this current at the point of the third or single eye. That is the connecting point between our soul in the body and the Light and Sound current emanating from the Creator. If we can concentrate our attention at that point, we can contact the Light and Sound current and soar on it back through the higher regions of existence. The current will ultimately lead us to our primary Source, back to the Lord.

 ## References to the Light and Sound in Religions

There is a startling similarity in the descriptions of the Light and Sound current given in various religious traditions. The creation account begins with God as the Power that brought all into being. This Power is called by different names, but its attributes are similar. For example, in the Bible, it is called the Word.

> *In the beginning was the Word, and the Word was with God, and the Word was God. The same was in the beginning with God. All things were made by Him, and without Him was not anything made that was made.*
>
> (John 1.1-3)

The ancient Greek philosophers called the power as "Logos." To them, "Logos" was the means by which God created the universe.

In the Old Testament, it is written:

> *He spoke and it was done.*
>
> (Psalm 33. 6,9)

> *Upholding all things by the Word of His Power.*
>
> (Hebrews 1.3)

> *The grass withereth, the flower fadeth, but the Word of God shall stand forever.*
>
> (Isaiah 40.8)

*And God said, Let there be light, and there was light.*

(Genesis 1.3)

In Hinduism, the Word is referred to as *Nad* or *Akash Bani* (the Voice coming down from the heavens), *Udgit*, *Jyoti* and *Sruti* (Light and Sound), or *prakash*. There are references to the Word in the Vedas and Upanishads:

*He has taken the support of the Word, the melodious tune.*

In Islam, the Sufis refer to the Light and Sound current or Word as *Sultan-ul-Azkar*, (the King of Prayers), *Saut-i-Sarmadi* (the Divine Song), *Nida-i-Asman* (the Heavenly Sound), *Kalam-i-Qadim* (the Ancient Sound) and the *Kalma* (Talk) or Word.

Shamas Tabrez has said, "Creation came into being from Saut (Sound or Word) and from Saut spread all light."[1]

In Sikhism, there are numerous references to the creative power of the Word. It is referred to as Naam or Shabd:

*The Word made all the earthly and heavenly systems.*

(Guru Granth Sahib, Gauri M.5)

In the Prologue to the Jap Ji, by Guru Nanak, it is written:

*There is One Reality, the Unmanifest-Manifested;*
*Ever-existent, He is Naam (Conscious Spirit);*
*The Creator pervading all;*
*Without fear, without enmity;*
*The timeless, the Unborn and the Self-existent,*
*Complete within itself.*

(Jap Ji Prologue)

Guru Amar Das has said, "He is in all Himself and revels in His creation by supporting it by Shabd" (Guru Granth Sahib, Majh M.3).

The Zoroastrians speak of Sraosha or Creative Verbum. In the Zoroastrian tradition we have:

> *Wherein the Omniscient, Self-existent Life-Giver dwells by His all-pervading Reality,*
> *I cause to invoke that divine Sraosha (i.e. the Word) which is the greatest of all divine gifts for spiritual succour.*
>
> (HA 33-35, Ahuravaiti Yasna)

Other saints have also spoken of the Sound current. Soami Shiv Dayal Singh has said:

> *The Sound or the Word is the prime cause of all. It is also the be-all and the end-all.*[2]

> *The Word and the spirit are of the same origin and both spring from the same essence of the Nameless One. It is both the cause and the effect, and all were created by It. The Word is the preceptor, as well as the disciple, and is resounding in the heart of all.*[3]

One who has come in contact with the Light and Sound can recognize the true meaning of references to it in the scriptures. Oftentimes, scriptures are couched in allegorical and metaphorical language to avoid giving away the full secret oral tradition to the masses. Only those who were privy to the oral tradition passed on from master to disciple knew the hidden meaning in the scriptural references. Once we understand the language, the meaning becomes clear and we are able to identify the descriptions of the attributes of the creative force mentioned in each scripture.

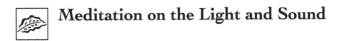 ## Meditation on the Light and Sound

Meditation on the Light and Sound consists of two practices: meditation on the inner Light and meditation on the inner Sound. Both practices have as their ultimate goal a conscious contact with the current of Light and Sound, leading to the soul rising above physical body-consciousness and traveling in the inner realms.

## ☉ Activity ☉

When meditating on the inner Light, we focus our attention at the third or single eye. At the same time, we repeat the names of God to occupy our mind and contact the Light already within us. The following describes the steps for this meditation practice:

Sit in a comfortable position in which our body can remain still for the longest possible time. It does not require any difficult asanas or poses; just choose a pose that is most comfortable in which we can sit longer. Meditation can be practiced in the comfort of our own home, in the office, while traveling in a bus, train, or airplane, or in a scenic spot outdoors. We need not leave our hearth and home to go into a jungle, a mountaintop, or cave to meditate. It is something that can be practiced wherever we are. We may sit on a chair, a sofa, or on the floor. We can even practice meditation lying down, but this is not recommended as it is easy to fall asleep in this position. But if we are ill or have a physical disability that does not permit us to sit, we can meditate lying down, as well.

Once we select a pose, we close our eyes. That which sees the darkness is not our outer eyes, rather, it is our inner eye or the eye of the soul. We then look into the middle of the field of darkness lying in front of us. When we look into the middle, our attention is actually focused horizontally with the physical eyes, about eight to ten inches in front of us. We should not try to lift our eyeballs upward toward our forehead in the hopes of

seeing something there because that puts strain on the
eyes and may result in a headache. Rather, we should
gaze comfortably with our eyes relaxed as we do when
we go to sleep.

Initially, we see darkness. But if we continue to gaze
in front of us, Light will sprout forth. We may see Lights
of various colors: red, yellow, orange, blue, green, purple,
white, or gold. We may see an inner vista such as stars,
moon, or sun. Whatever we see, we should continue
gazing into the center. Ultimately, we will find our
attention so absorbed in the inner vista that we begin to
rise above body-consciousness and soar into the regions
Beyond.

In the meditation on the inner Sound, we listen to
the Sound coming to us from within. The Sound current
comes from above and ultimately pulls our soul within
on a journey into the Beyond.

∞

## References to Meditation in Different Religions

Both of these forms of meditation have been practiced by saints and
mystics in different religions. Because the terminology used for the Light
and Sound current differs in various languages and cultures, we may
think they are different practices. But the underlying practices used
around the world are basically the same.

For example, in the Bible, this Light and Sound current is called the
holy Word.

> *By hearing, ye shall hear, and shall not understand,*
> *and seeing ye shall see, and shall not perceive.*
>
> (Matt. 13.14)

> *But blessed are your eyes, for they see; and your ears, for they*
> *hear. For verily I say unto you, That many prophets and*
> *righteous men have desired to see those things which ye see, and*
> *have not seen them; and to hear those things which ye heard,*
> *and have not heard them.*
>
> (Matt. 13.16-17)

The Light and Sound current is subtle. It cannot be perceived by our physical eyes and ears. It is something that we see and hear with the eye of the soul. So when the Bible tells us that "by hearing, ye shall hear" it is saying that the Word is not heard with our physical hearing mechanism, but with the attention of our soul. When we see the inner Light, it is neither registered on our retina nor conveyed along our optic nerve to the brain; rather, it is seen at the level of the soul.

In the Sikh tradition, Guru Nanak has said:

> *Know ye the true knowledge and meditation to be the Sound*
>   *Divine,*
> *Blessed is the evergreen tree with the immense shade.*

The Upanishads say that "Meditation on Nad or the Sound Principle is the royal road to salvation" (Hansa Naad Upanishad).

Maulana Rumi, a Sufi saint, has said, "Grow not skeptical, but attune thyself to the sound coming down from the heavens." He has also said, "Rise above the horizon, O brave soul, and hear the melodious song coming from the highest heaven."

Prophet Mohammed said, "The Voice of God comes unto my ears as any other sounds."

In the Jain scriptures, it is written:

> *The aspirant is enjoined to sit in solitude and meditate with a*
> *single-pointed attention, on the Maha Mantra of Panch*
> *permesti and to perceive the Light.*

> (Shri Sutra Nandi)

If we can meditate on the inner Light and Sound we will find that we can reach our goal. We begin our concentration at the third eye because it is from there that the soul leaves the body. Since the current of Light and Sound flows from God, we can catch its celestial music and like a stream follow it back to its source.

## How We Can Keep Our Mind Stilled During Meditation

The mind is in continuous motion. The harder we try to keep the mind still, the more thoughts it sends to us. The mind is like mercury; it is always restless and always moving. It can jump from images and thoughts of New York, to Paris, to Delhi, and back again. Saints and mystics have grappled with this problem throughout the ages. Many scriptures speak of occupying the mind with a task to keep it busy: repetition of the Lord's name. Repetition keeps the mind occupied so that our attention can focus its gaze on the field of vision lying in front of us.

There are some who practice this repetition orally. Some say the names of God while turning beads. Others do it by sitting still, but with their tongue moving. The most efficient way is to repeat the names of God mentally. The concept behind the mental repetition is to keep the body stilled. If the tongue is moving, the attention will be on the brain moving the tongue. Using the tongue also means that the sound of the names will be audible, which will activate our attention to the sense of hearing. Mental repetition, however, does not involve any organs or senses. The mouth is still, and the sense of hearing is not activated. In mental repetition, only thought is occupied, which is precisely the point—to keep it busy. One repeats the names of God, thus stilling the mind. While the mind is quiet, our attention can then focus at the third eye without disturbance so we can see the inner Light of God.

The words used in repetition are sometimes called a mantra. Mantras have been used since ancient times, selected by saints or masters who were adept in the power of sound beyond the human ken. These sacred syllables, when charged with the spiritual attention of an enlightened being, have the power to attract the attention to the point where it can contact the Light and Sound. The charging helps the aspirant to focus the attention at the third eye. It helps us to withdraw our attention from the world and the body and to focus at the third eye. The repetition of the names gives a spiritual boost to the soul so that it can withdraw from consciousness of the body and connect with the Light and Sound within us and ultimately enter a state of consciousness of the realms Beyond.

Through meditation, a whole new world opens up for us. By learning meditation, we can gain entry through a doorway that leads us to worlds of bliss, light, and love within.

# Journey to Realms of Light Within Us

Regions of Light that embrace souls with a powerful love await each one of us within. Sights and sounds beyond anything we could ever imagine reside within us. Incredible music far beyond any that can be produced by worldly instruments is reverberating at every moment. Realms in which love resounds exist within at this very moment. Colors we could never imagine and sounds so melodious they enchant the soul characterize the inner realms. Places of bliss and joy from which all our worldly cares are forgotten call to us from within.

We know that those who have had near-death experiences have encountered even at the borders of the beyond a light more brilliant than any seen on earth. They speak of a being of Light that radiates so much love that it was greater than any they had known in this world. Books by Dr. Raymond Moody and personal accounts by Bette Eadie and numerous others who have had a near-death experience give us an inkling of what awaits us within. We do not need a near-death experience to encounter the inner realms, but we can enter the doorway through meditation.

**How Do We Know about the Inner Realms?**

There is an inner cosmogony of spiritual realms mapped out for us by explorers who have visited them. While the terminology they have used to describe these realms differs, their experiences are the same. Since different terms are used, people may feel they are not the same place. Let us take an analogy from this world. Let us suppose that three people— one from France, one from India, and one from America—take a trip to Kashmir. The person from France visiting Kashmir may talk about the flowers he sees there and call them "les fleurs," the person from India may call them "phul," and the visitor from America may call them "flowers." The sights are the same, but the words used to describe them differ. Now, suppose each of these travelers records what he or she saw in a printed journal. Someone from another country who speaks neither English, French, nor Hindi reads the accounts. Without knowing the languages and without having been to Kashmir, the reader may think that the travelers each visited different places. Only an experienced traveler who had also been to Kashmir could point out that the three travelers from France, India, and America were referring to the same sight but simply using different terminology. It is the same with travel in the inner regions. Each explorer may have come from a different country and may have spoken a different language. Thus, years or centuries later, when we read their accounts, we may not realize they were visiting the same place.

Another problem with describing the inner regions is how to divide them. For example, one inner traveler may divide them by certain characteristics and demarcation lines and come up with five inner regions, while another may divide them by different characteristics and come up with eight regions. A third person may divide them into three, while someone else may lump them all into one. How does this happen? Let us again use an analogy from world travel. Suppose we visit Niagara Falls, which sits on the border between the United States and Canada.

Someone without a map may not realize that there is a demarcation line between the two countries and thinks that both sides of the falls belong to the same country. Since there are no road maps of the inner regions nor street markers, travelers to the regions within may count the number of regions differently.

The descriptions that we have from the writings of past explorers are extremely interesting and may serve to inspire us to take the same inner voyage. But the proof of their existence can only be confirmed when we take the journey ourselves. No amount of writings will satisfy a seeker of truth unless he or she sees with his or her own eyes and hears with his or her own ears. In this age of scientific proof, people want their own experience to verify the truth of statements made by others. We may read what others have experienced within, but our thirst will only be truly satisfied when we drink of the inner nectar ourselves and find out with our own inner eyes and ears what lies beyond. As we read what saints and mystics have experienced in the beyond, we need to keep in mind that through meditation we can prove their statements and experience the truth for ourselves.

## Descriptions of the Inner Regions

A detailed cosmology of the inner regions has come from several sources. If we compare the Hindu Puranas, the mystical writings found in Christianity and Judaism, and the writings of the saints of the East from several traditions, we get a profile of inner regions beyond the physical one. While accounts in other religions may not be as detailed, there are descriptions of portions of the inner realms that match these accounts. Unfortunately, many of the saints, mystics, prophets, and religious founders did not all record their inner experiences in their totality or did not record them at all. Some saints and mystics did not leave behind any writings. Thus, if a religion was founded after these saints left the world, and the saint did not leave any record of the inner regions, followers may have assumed that because nothing was said, the regions do not exist. Another possibility is that followers believe the inner realms exist only so far as the descriptions left behind. For example, in some religions, there are descriptions of heaven. But if only heaven is described and not the other spiritual realms, followers may think the only region that exists is that particular heaven.

We have a similar problem when we read the history of the world. The historical accounts we find in books are subjective. If the historian chose to leave out certain portions of history, it does not mean that those events did not occur. Thus, as we look through the accounts of the inner regions described by saints, mystics, prophets, and spiritual teachers, we need to keep in mind that each described the regions to the extent that he or she wished to or felt were important to followers. Those who did not leave a record behind did not necessarily mean to imply that these inner realms do not exist.

Many saints believed that the inner spiritual realms were not for the masses and kept the information secret, to be passed orally only from master to disciple. The ancient Greek Mystery schools were a good example of this. They revealed "mysteries" only to initiates. But some of the students of these mystery schools, such as Plato and Socrates, did make reference to the spiritual mysteries in their writings. Some of the saints, such as Kabir and Soami Shiv Dayal Singh, did leave behind detailed records. Although they kept some of the teachings secret for their disciples only, they did relay much about the inner cosmogony to the masses.

A composite of the inner regions compiled from many of these sources shows a progression of regions, described either from the physical realm ascending to the spiritual realms or starting with the spiritual realms and descending to the physical one. In the Bible, Jesus says:

> *In my Father's house there are many mansions.*
>
> (John 14.2-3)

The following describes the cosmogony from the standpoint of a soul who rises above body-consciousness through meditation.

When we focus our attention at the third or single eye, we can pick up the current of Light and Sound. The soul, absorbed in that current, begins to transcend physical consciousness of the body and the world. As we are absorbed in the inner Light, we pass through a vista of inner stars, moon, and sun, and come to the gateway of the astral realm. We reach the astral region from which Light and Sound stream forth. Our soul, having shed its physical body, now travels in a lighter, more ethereal body, known as an astral body. The astral region, although not as solid as our physical plane, has many similar features to this world but in a finer and more subtler form. It has a brighter light than this region, and the region is permeated with the beautiful music of the Sound current that manifests as its own distinct sound. Unfortunately, it is easy for a traveling soul to get captivated and caught up in this region. It is filled with numerous temptations that are much easier to satisfy than those of the physical plane because we are not encumbered by the obstacle of a physical body. As quickly as thoughts materialize, we can move from one area of the astral region to another, gratifying one desire after another. It is by no means a spiritual region, and the soul can get lost in its never-ending supply of pleasures. Saints and mystics try to keep their disciples from getting lost in this region, and prefer to guide the soul further on to the higher planes, shielding them from these distractions.

The soul travels next from the astral region to the causal region. The causal plane has its own distinguishing Light and Sound, much brighter and more melodious than those found in the astral region. It is in this region that the soul functions with a causal body and a causal mind much more ethereal than the astral body and astral mind and is one with the Universal Mind. While this is a fascinating prospect—having knowledge of all the workings of the three lower regions—it, too, carries a great danger for the soul. The power of the mind is so great that we can become lost in its knowledge. We can be caught up in a state of endless creativity, devising new inventions, creating in the realms of music, poetry, fine arts, dance, sculpture, and literary works. Many creations in the physical world are the result of inspiration from the causal regions of the Universal Mind. That is how a scientist, writer, poet, or an artist can emerge from sleep or a reverie with sudden inspiration to solve a problem or create. Think of the endless permutations and combinations of creations. From a set number of musical notes, the mind can create countless songs and tunes. From a set number of letters, sounds, and words the mind can create a seemingly endless number of writings and spoken thoughts. From a set palette of colors, one can create numerous paintings. Walk through any shopping mall and see the stream of products. Whatever is in the physical world comes from the mind, whose home lies in the causal region. As it is said in the Hindu scriptures about this region, "What is here (the phenomenal world), the same is there (in Brahman); and what is there, the same is here" (Katha Upanishad 2.1.10).

Again, it is dangerous for the soul to get caught up in the causal region. True, it is a beautiful region, even more subtle than the astral and physical regions. But if the soul gets caught up in the mind's knowledge, it can have great difficulty rising higher.

A spiritual guide is important to ensure that the soul does not get caught in this region. The Universal Mind makes every effort to keep the soul in its clutches, for the next region is the spiritual realm, in which the soul regains its consciousness of who it is. It is only with the guidance of an experienced inner traveler that we can avoid the pitfalls that face us in the astral and causal regions. The inner explorer who knows the way will take us to a region called the supracausal region, instead of letting us get lost in the causal region. In the supracausal region, we find a pool of nectar, called the Mansarovar, in which the soul bathes and sheds its causal body. The soul is now covered only with its supracausal body, which is but a thin veil surrounding the soul. This region is beyond the mind and senses. There is absolutely no physical language that can describe the supracausal realm. We have only pale analogies. Since the physical, astral, and causal minds have been left behind in the lower worlds, the mind is of no help to us here. It is an experience of the soul. The supracausal plane also has its own distinguishing Light and Sound that help the soul recognize where it is. It is in this plane that the soul, losing its previous forgetfulness of its true nature, realizes, "I am the same essence as God."

The soul, though, realizes there is still a veil separating it from the Lord. An intense desire emerges in the soul to reunite with its Beloved. It does not want to linger in the supracausal region; the call of the Lord is great. The soul wants to venture further to find the waiting arms of its Beloved Lord. Continuing further, the soul finally enters the purely spiritual region of Sach Khand or Sat Lok (True Region), its eternal Home. With intensity far greater than a worldly lover has for its Beloved, the soul rushes into the arms of the Lord. Like iron filings to a magnet, the soul is pulled to reunite with God. The joys of the eternal Home reach an intensity beyond human thought. The soul enters a state of eternal bliss as it merges with God in this region. It is with exhilaration and joyousness that the soul experiences its own true state here. A sense of freedom fills the soul, and it exists in a state of pure delight and wonder. Although this is a pale analogy, think of the sense of freedom and peace we feel when we are on holiday or vacation. We turn off our alarm clocks, lock away our day-timers, and just enjoy a timeless state of relaxation and enjoyment. Here, the soul finds its eternal rest from the pains, sorrows, temptations, and disappointments of the lower regions. There is no pain, sorrow, or death here. All is joyousness, love, and perpetual happiness. Souls eternally enjoy their oneness with the Lord. The soul has been empowered. Here, we enter a state of unlimited divine wisdom, immortality, unconditional love, fearlessness, connectedness, and bliss. It is here that we exist as a completely empowered soul.

.

# Removing the Coverings of the Soul 13

A mountain climbing team ascending a Himalayan peak has to remain focused to achieve its goal. Similarly, when we try to rise above body-consciousness, our soul must be focused on the goal. To withdraw our attention to the sixth chakra, we cannot have any interference from our mind or body. If we move our body, our concentration is disturbed. If we have thoughts, our mind disturbs the concentration of our attention.

One blockage that is the root cause of slowing our progress is distraction during meditation caused by our negative thoughts, words, and deeds throughout the day.

Distracting thoughts due to anger, falsehood, lust, greed, attachment, and ego swirl about in our mind like a tornado during the time we are trying to meditate. If we can eliminate these negative traits, or learn to control them, our mind will be more balanced and calm, and our meditation will improve.

If we can eliminate this blockage, our mind will be in the calm and peaceful state necessary for successful meditation, and we will put an end to the layers of anger that add dark spots and hide the luminosity of our soul.

 ## Becoming Aware of Our Blockages

The first step in removing the blockages that cover our soul is to become aware of them. When we go to a doctor, we cannot be cured until a proper diagnosis is made. When we go to a teacher, an evaluation must be made of our current abilities before it is known what skills we need to be taught. When we go to a sports coach, our abilities must be analyzed before we can be guided on how to improve. Similarly, we must know what blockages we have in order to begin the work of removing them.

Many saints, mystics, and philosophers of the past made a systematic effort to analyze their own blockages. Each day, they would review their thoughts, words, and deeds committed throughout that day. If they found they failed in the various ethical virtues, they made a resolution to improve the following day. Khwaja Hafiz, a Persian mystic, would drop a small pebble into an earthen pitcher for each of his failures. After several days, he would be distressed if he found the pitcher had completely filled up. In India, some of the wise ones would throw small kernels of grain into a pitcher each time they failed in virtuous behavior. Or they would tie a knot in their clothing for each failure and at the end of the day count the knots. The Christian saint, St. Ignatius Loyola, suggested that every day people should analyze their faults. He recommended that we ask God to help us recall how many times we committed a certain fault each day and ask God's forgiveness. Then, we should try to guard against committing that fault the following day.

Reviewing our failures is like looking in a mirror to see what blemishes we have. If we list the various categories, such as nonviolence, truthfulness, purity, humility, and selfless service, and each day count the number of failures we have in each category in thought, word, and deed, we would have a profile of what blockages are keeping us from empowering our soul. We should not do this self-analysis with an eye to chastise ourselves, however, but to improve on the following day. This should not serve as food for depression and low self-esteem; rather the analysis should be a tool to help us see what areas we need to work on in order to meet our spiritual goal.

Once we know where we stand as far as our current blockages go, we can then take steps to eliminate them. We may wish to keep a record and follow our progress over time. We can aim for zero failures in the various categories of virtues, but we should not expect to eliminate them all at once. Change takes time. Old habits die hard. Our progress may be gradual, and that is all right. We may start out with incremental changes, such as one, two, three, or four improvements in a category each day. Or we may wish to start with one category at a time and concentrate on only improving in that area first before going on to other areas. It does not matter how we improve, as long as each day sees some incremental progress. The climb up a mountain takes place one step at a time. If we think we are going to fly to the top in an instant, we may become disappointed and discouraged because we have set unrealistic goals. Rather than becoming disheartened and giving up, it is better to take small steps at a time and find that we are progressing gradually. Before we know it, a day will come when we will find we have reduced failures in many categories.

So let us begin by analyzing where we stand. Let us be honest in looking at ourselves. If we try to cover up our shortcomings, no one but ourselves will be hurt in the process. We delay our own progress by ignoring our blemishes. The more honest we can be in looking at ourselves, the sooner we can take action to rectify our failures and start to eliminate them.

## Eliminating the Blockage of Anger

We may think that no one knows what we are thinking, but our thoughts produce vibrations that can be picked up by others at a subtle level. For example, Akbar was an Emperor of India. Once, one of Akbar's ministers advised him to be careful about what he thinks of others. The minister said, "Thoughts are very potent. Let us try this experiment. See that man coming down the road? As he approaches, I want you to think angry thoughts about him and let us see what happens."

The emperor looked at the stranger and thought, "This stranger should be beaten."

When the stranger drew near, Akbar asked him, "What did you think when you saw my face."

"Excuse me, Emperor, but I wanted to beat you and break your head."

No words were spoken; no actions were done, but the angry thoughts of Akbar toward the man were picked up, and the stranger was tempted to react in a violent way. We may not say anything, but our anger may result in a negative vibration in the environment through aggressive body language, facial gestures, and angry tones of voice. This not only affects the recipient of our anger, but boomerangs back on us, disturbing our own peace of mind.

The result of our anger is that when we sit for meditation, we relive the angry incident. We replay our angry actions or ruminate over our angry words and thoughts. We continue to react and be upset over what happened. We may spend a lot of time thinking about how we are going to get even with the person, take revenge, or retaliate. We may plan how to solve the problem, and what steps we will take to protect ourselves next time. The precious time we had planned to spend in meditation is eaten away by thinking over what happened in the past that made us angry and what we could do in the future as a solution.

We can eliminate anger by replacing it with nonviolence. We are faced daily with numerous situations that can upset us. Things do not go our way. People do not do what we want, and they say things that hurt us. To respond with anger only perpetuates the negativity. The cycle of "I hurt you" and "you hurt me" continues unbroken. The only way to break the cycle is through nonviolence. We need to take control of our mind and respond differently. It may be difficult, but it is not impossible. Christ said, "And unto him that smiteth thee on the one cheek offer also the other" (Luke 6.29). Mahatma Gandhi, through nonviolent means, helped to gain India's independence from Britain. Dr. Martin Luther King, Jr. led the civil rights movement in the United States through nonviolent means. Each knew that violence begat violence, and if a humane, peaceful world was to be realized, it could only be achieved through nonviolence.

We can deal with anger in several ways. One way is to project out the long-term consequences of our anger as a deterrent. Another approach is to set a goal and then realize the effect that anger may have in preventing us from attaining that goal. A third way is to use meditation to break the physiological response to anger.

Projecting the future consequences of our anger can prevent us from acting with anger. Suppose someone has aroused our anger. We can train ourselves to stop the anger by saying to ourselves, "If we continue to have angry thoughts, speak angry words, or act violently, then we are not helping ourselves." Or we can say, "If I continue in this state of anger, I will be creating problems for myself." We may wish to even say, "That person has hurt me and has created problems for himself or herself in doing so. Do I wish to respond in anger and add to my own problems?" By becoming conscious of the effect our anger will have, we may be able to train our mind to respond nonviolently to situations, as did Lord Buddha when someone hurled a barrage of angry abusive remarks on him one day. He listened patiently, although some of his disciples were distressed and wished to retaliate against the attacker. Instead, Lord Buddha said to the heckler, "Your gift I do not accept." Thus, the gift of anger brought by the abuser remained with him and had no effect on Lord Buddha at all.

Another way to control our anger is to set a goal. If we set a goal to meditate a certain number of hours a day to achieve spiritual progress, then we can guard against intrusion on that time. If we feel ourselves getting angry, we can say to ourselves, "If I allow this anger to take control of me, then it is going to cause me to waste my precious meditation time. Rather than meditating, I will end up sitting and thinking about how angry I am. In such a state, how can I calmly meditate and focus on what I am seeing within? The anger may rankle within me for hours or days, thus causing me to waste what little time I have available for meditation." We may extend this thought further to say, "There are always going to be situations that may make me angry. Do I wish to go through my life being angry about one thing or another? This life is precious—I do not want to waste it on unnecessary anger that will not help me."

Another way to deal with anger is through meditation. It sounds like a catch-22 situation: to have fruitful meditation we need to overcome anger, but to overcome anger we need to meditate. It is not so much a catch-22 situation, however, as it is a cycle of success. No matter what level of meditation we are at, the time we spend meditating can calm us down so that we do not respond to a situation in anger. Meditation provides us with a physiological response to control the anger. Our heartbeat slows during meditation, which has the corresponding effect of slowing down our brain waves. We enter a more relaxed state of body and mind. In such a state, anger has less chance to gain strength. As we calm down and our anger subsides, we can increase our concentration in meditation. The more time we spend in meditation, the more practiced we are in being calm and balanced.

## Eliminating the Blockage of Falsehood

Another avenue through which we can speed our spiritual advancement is the elimination of falsehood. Falsehood is a trap into which our mind leads us. If we tell a lie, deceive others, steal, or hide the truth, our mind will be occupied in perpetuating the falsehood. We will have to spend time worrying about how to prevent ourselves from being caught. For each lie or dishonest act we commit, we have to spin many others to cover it up. We have to keep track of what we told this person and that one so that we are not caught in our lie. The worry and fear may rankle in our heads, disturbing our peace of mind during meditation. If we are honest and truthful at all times, we have nothing to hide and nothing to fear. If we are honest in our dealings, we need not worry about someone tracking what we have done. We can sleep peacefully and meditate peacefully.

There are several ways to eliminate falsehood from our lives. One way is to realize that while we may hide from others for a time, God knows what we do, and our actions are impeccably registered within our soul. We cannot hide from God what we do. We may temporarily pull the wool over the eyes of others, but God is truth, and when we deal in untruths we are far from the Lord. Whatever we think we are getting away with will catch up with us. If we think before we act, we can save ourselves much heartache later.

If we set for ourselves the goal of empowering the soul, then we do not want to put any obstacles in our way. If we recognize that leading a life of falsehood is going to make us a slave to many more lies, we may think twice before lying, stealing, and deceiving. Our life will no longer be in the service of our soul and the Lord, but to our lie. The time spent in protecting the lie will take us away from the state of equanimity needed for meditation. During the day, instead of occupying ourselves with thoughts of love, truth, and service, we will be haunted by our untruth. Do we wish to waste the precious breaths given to us by serving falsehood? Thinking about our goal and working zealously toward achieving it can help us guard against falling into the pitfall of falsehood.

 ## Eliminating the Blockage of Lust

Another blockage that we need to eliminate is lust. Lust takes us in the opposite direction of discovering our soul. We know how the mind and senses are dragged into the temptations of the world. When we allow this to happen, we are like the child on the carousel who passes the golden ring but misses it every time. The golden ring is waiting at the sixth chakra. If our attention is diverted by lust, we will not catch the ring. Lust only delays our progress. Can we afford to waste time in reaching the doorway that leads us to the soul and God?

There are several ways to overcome lust. One is to understand the dangers of falling into lust's snares. Another is to stick to our chosen goals. A third way is to replace lust with purity and the greater enjoyments found within during meditation.

It may be difficult, but if we can take control and think about what we are doing before falling into lust's pitfalls, we may avoid the danger. If we are in danger of becoming addicted to drugs or alcohol, we may wish to consider the impact on our physical body or on the lives of our loved ones and get help. Some people have an addiction to lustful pursuits and lose themselves in sensual pleasures. Those addictions may cause injury to others who do not wish to be party to such acts. The very pain we may think we are trying to avoid through our addictions will return to us later and may be manifold more if we are hurting others in some way.

Engaging in lust of any kind can hinder our progress. The greater enjoyments waiting within elude us if we become entrapped in the enjoyments of this world. The pleasures of this world are transitory. We are throwing away the opportunity for lasting and permanent bliss and happiness and opting for bubbles that can burst in a moment when we become entrapped by lust.

How can we replace lust with purity? If we surround ourselves with people and places in which lust has a stronghold, our temptations can be great. If we replace these with people and environments imbued with purity, we face less temptation. We can keep our mind engaged in pure thoughts by reading scriptures, listening to devotional music, or going to places where we can be devoted to God. Talking about spiritual topics and God can help keep us engaged in purity of word. Being involved in acts of selfless service to others, engaging in activities that improve our physical health or develop our mind, skills, and talents, may help keep our mind pure.

The best method, though, for overcoming lust is to replace the worldly pleasures with a spiritual pleasure. When a child has a plaything that we want to remove from his or her hand, we can do this best by replacing the object with something more enjoyable. The bliss we receive from connecting the soul with God is so much more satisfying, fulfilling, and intoxicating than anything in this world. Spending time in meditation can provide us with a method for keeping our attention away from lustful pursuits. Each time we meditate, our soul is being empowered. As we empower it more and more, it comes to our aid in facing worldly temptations. God aids our soul in empowering us to deal with lust. We then are better able to concentrate on our meditations. As we gain more in meditation, we are further strengthened. With renewed strength, our soul can control our mind and its lusts. The cycle continues until we ultimately overcome the blockage of lust and experience far greater ecstasy within us.

## Overcoming the Blockage of Greed

Greed keeps us on a never-ending treadmill. It leads us from the pursuit of one worldly acquisition to another without allowing us to feel satisfied. We can have greed for money, possessions, power, or fame. No matter what we have, we desire more of it, or something entirely different. The result is that our energy is spent in protecting that which we have or in acquiring that which we do not yet have. We become so preoccupied with trying to satisfy our greed, that there is little time and energy left for realizing our soul.

How can we eliminate the blockage of greed? To do so, we need to develop right understanding. We need to understand that what we are trying to hold on to or grasp in this world is as impermanent as a child's sand castle. The ocean of life can wash it away with the incoming tides, taking with it that which we have worked so hard to build. Through meditation, however, we can taste the permanent riches awaiting us within.

King Mahmud of Ghazni built his empire by conquering the people of Asia. He had accrued treasures from all over his kingdom, yet before he died, he asked that everything that he amassed be displayed for him to see. For several hours he looked at gold coins, precious jewels, and priceless objects. Suddenly, he began to cry. He told his courtiers, "I have slain tens of thousands of people, causing thousands of women to be widowed and children orphaned for these objects. Yet not even the smallest piece of gold can go with me now that I am about to die." He then asked his courtiers that when they take his body to the burial place they should extend both his hands outside of the coffin. When asked why he wished to do so, he replied, "I wish to let people know that with all my wealth, I was leaving the world empty-handed. We cannot take anything material of this world with us." Each time we desire something of this world, let us take a moment and think of its cost to us. As Christ said:

> *What does it profit a man to gain possession of the world, if one loses one's soul.*

(Mark 8.36)

Greed can be replaced with detachment. While working hard to earn a livelihood, some people amass great earnings while others make a meager salary. Whatever we receive we should accept in a spirit of detachment without becoming greedy. One can try for positions to make more money or put in more time to earn overtime and still be detached from the results. We can make use of whatever we earn to feed, clothe, and house our family and ourselves, and share with others in need. But what we have should not be the object of our attachment. What we have arouses our greed if we spend all our time obsessively worrying about it, or when we hoard to keep what we have. If we use illegal means to gain more, or if we try to take from others what is rightfully theirs, it not only is a violation of truthfulness, it is an expression of greed.

The riches we amass during our lifetime cannot go with us to the Beyond; but the record of our deeds during our lifetime does. Do we wish to trade away our innate goodness for transitory possessions? By understanding that what is reality is our soul and God and that what is transitory is the world, we can make better choices and begin to control greed.

Another way to eliminate greed is to analyze its cost to our soul. An anecdote from the life of Abou ben Adham illustrates this point. Abou ben Adham (known as Ebrahim ibn Adham) was the king of Balkh when an incident occurred that aroused self-searching about his aim in life. While sitting on his throne with his ministers on either side, he gave audience to the masses. Suddenly, a man approached him. He had such a terrifying expression that even the king's ministers did not want to look at this stranger.

"What do you want?" asked Abou.

"I am only stopping off at this inn," replied the stranger.

"This is not an inn. This is my palace. You must be a madman," replied the king.

"Who owned this palace before you?" asked the man.

"My father," said Abou.

"And who owned it before him?" asked the man.

"My grandfather," responded Abou. The dialogue proceeded further with the stranger continuing to ask who owned the palace prior to the last one mentioned.

Finally, the stranger said, "To where have all these owners departed?"

"They are all dead," said Abou.

"Then," concluded the stranger, "is this not an inn in which one person enters and another leaves?" With this statement, the stranger disappeared. This exchange started Abou ben Adham on his search for God, as he realized that the things of this world were transitory and that what was more important to him was finding his soul and God.

In order to realize our self and realize God, we know that it takes time and attention. We need to spend time in meditation; we need to eliminate the various blockages by leading a positive life of love; we need to think about what greed will cost us in terms of achieving our goal.

Can we replace greed? The joy of giving can surpass the happiness of receiving. In return, we can receive far more than we give. The blessings that become ours for giving and sharing cannot be measured on earth; we are showered with God's love and grace. When we find ourselves in the clutches of greed, we can consider doing a selfless act in its place. Over time, a new habit can form, and we can begin to look for opportunities for giving rather than taking.

Whenever we feel we desire more objects and possessions, we are losing control of ourselves. To regain our balance, we can sit in meditation. As we contact the Light and Sound and venture above body-consciousness, we realize the impermanent nature of this world and the permanent nature of our soul. We experience our soul beyond the physical body. With that new perspective, we can look at the objects of this world as temporary bubbles that vanish in the twinkling of an eye. We realize that what is important is our soul and God. We come to see that what matters in the Beyond is how much we give of ourselves to others selflessly.

By developing a selfless, giving attitude we can find that the spots covering our soul due to greed begin to fall away. Our spiritual progress can advance much further each time we empower our soul to give and share.

## Overcoming the Blockage of Attachment

Attachment creates a blockage for the soul because it pulls our attention into the world. As citizens of this physical universe we need physical belongings, family relationships, and material objects that are necessary for survival. It goes with the territory of being a human being. What is harmful to our spiritual progress is being so attached that it distracts us from our spiritual goal. We may have a family, a house, furniture, a car, clothing, a bank account, and whatever is necessary for modern life, but if we are so attached to them that we do not give any attention to our soul and our spiritual progress, then they become a source of bondage. If we wish to empower our soul, we need to live in a state of detachment. This means that we use the things we have been given or have earned but remain detached so they do not occupy so much of our attention that we forget our soul.

The way to overcome attachment is to develop detachment. We need to be like the lotus that lives in muddy waters but whose petals remain unsullied. Detachment means that we live in this world, but we are able to rise above it when necessary to connect our soul with God.

The things to which we are attached in this world cannot go with us beyond the borders of this life. This realization can help us focus our attention on the spiritual side of our life, for what we gain in the realm of the soul will be with us forever.

The main problem with attachment is that it leads to other negative qualities. If we are too attached to something, we may get angry at anyone who tries to take it away from us. To hold on to that which we are attached, we may enter into deceit or falsehood. When we want more of those things to which we are attached, we may enter into greed. Obsessive attachment may lead to lust. We may be proud of our belongings and add to our ego. Being aware of the pitfalls of attachment and how it can add more and more layers to our soul can help us to stay clear of this obstacle. Detachment helps free us to pursue God through meditation, to lead a life of positive qualities, and to realize our soul.

## Overcoming the Blockage of Ego

One of the subtlest and trickiest blockages to overcome is the ego. Ego is the mind's way of keeping us from having contact with our spiritual nature. Ego manifests in several forms: pride of wealth, pride of knowledge, pride of beauty, and pride of power. The harm caused by the ego is that it boosts up our mental and physical attributes, worldly positions, and possessions while it negates God, who is the true Giver of these gifts. By thinking too much of ourselves we forget that we are really a part of God, the one responsible for all the good that we are and all that we have. Another danger of the ego is that we can hurt others by making them feel like we are better than them and that they are worthless. In hurting them, we end up hurting ourselves.

Ego is the hardest blockage to eliminate. Even rishis and seers who spent their lives doing penances found they could not give up their ego. If people who spend their life in devotion to God can not give up the ego, then how can a beginner on the spiritual way do so? A way to eliminate ego is to come in contact with the Light and Sound of God through meditation. Each time we meditate, the ego becomes less and less. Why? As we experience our soul and the inner Light and Sound we come to realize more of God's greatness. As our soul journeys through the spiritual regions within, we realize that we are a part of God and that whatever we are or have is all due to the Lord. If we are given a beautiful body, a good intellect, or position or wealth in life, it is all due to God's blessings. In place of being egoistic, we develop an attitude of thankfulness. Instead of being great-full, of full of our own greatness, we become grateful to God.

There is a wonderful story to illustrate this point. There was a holy man who spent his life doing penances to God. Each day, he knelt on the hard ground in prayer to the Lord. He prayed so diligently that his knees became pained from this position. As he lived in the desert, the only source of food was a pomegranate tree. Each day, the tree bore one fruit that the man used to drink its juice and eat the fruit. When the man's life came to an end, he was taken before God for judgment on what should become of him in the afterlife.

The Lord said to him, "I forgive you as a sign of grace." The man was shocked. He wondered why God is forgiving him since he spent his whole life kneeling in prayer to the Lord. He had expected God to show him great honor for his piety and holiness. Was there some mistake? he wondered.

The man finally said, "O God, I devoted my whole life in prayer to You. How is it that You are having to forgive me when I have done no sin?"

God said, "Do you want me to show you your sins?" The man was in disbelief because he had not recalled doing anything sinful in his life.

"Yes, I would like to know how I have sinned."

God said, "Each day that you walked to the place to do your prayers, you stepped on many insects and killed them." As God spoke, the man began to quiver in fear that God was going to punish him.

Proceeding further, God said, "You lived in a desert incapable of providing you any food, yet I caused one pomegranate tree to grow to provide you with food and drink, and you never offered any gratitude to Me for this."

The man, realizing his mistakes, pleaded with God for forgiveness.

God replied, "Now you understand that for all your sins, I forgive you as a sign of grace." The man, realizing his errors, bowed in gratitude to the Lord for His mercy.

This anecdote illustrates how subtle the ego it. Despite a life of seeming piety and holiness, the man was unconsciously committing mistakes. Ego arises when we think we are perfect or better than we are, and do not recognize in humility our weaknesses. We do not realize that despite our faults, God is merciful and provides us with what we need, whether we deserve it or not.

We can overcome our ego through meditation and witnessing more and more of God's greatness. We can also lessen the ego by practicing gratefulness to God for what we receive. When we realize that God is the giver and we are receivers, then we will be less likely to boost ourselves for our good qualities. We will accept the good that we have as God's gifts, and begin to develop humility. With this humility, we will also begin to see the good in others. We will be more forgiving and accepting of others and more forgiving of their mistakes for we will see that we too have failings. In this way, we can eliminate the blockage of ego and return to the natural state of humility that characterizes our soul.

 ## Introspection as a Tool to See Ourselves

## ⚮ Activity ⚮

By spending time daily in introspection about our thoughts, words, and deeds, we can see where we stand. We will find what blemishes mar our face and can then take steps to remove them. If we see that we have weak-nesses in certain areas, we can focus on overcoming them. Being conscious of our blockages is the first step. Then we can take steps to be aware of our thoughts, words, and deeds and try to control them. Slowly and steadily we will be able to remove each blockage, one by one. Through meditation, we can speed up the process by coming in contact with the source of all goodness. The cleansing power of the Light and Sound of God helps us eliminate negative qualities. In this way, our soul can shine with all its beauty, light, and love.

# Finding Time for Our Self

**14**

If someone were to tell us that somewhere in our backyard, deep in the ground, lay a buried treasure worth millions of dollars, what would we do? Where would we be in our every spare moment? We would probably be out there in our backyard, digging frantically until we found our pot of gold. How could we concentrate on anything else knowing that we were living on top of a gold mine? Yet, this situation is not far from what is actually happening to each of us. We have a buried treasure within us containing riches far more fulfilling than having millions of dollars. We have a way to connect with our Creator waiting to be found within us, yet we go about our lives oblivious to our limitless potential.

The happiness that we think can be attained through outer wealth is illusory. The reason we want money is to buy things, thinking those objects will give us happiness. Yet, look at the wealthy nations of the world. Are its people happy? If they were, why are so many people drowning their sorrows in drugs, alcohol, or destructive pastimes, or lying on the couches of therapists? Some of the people who have everything money can buy, plus fame and power, are often so miserable they even end their lives tragically by overdosing on drugs and alcohol. Apparently, the money, fame, and position are not offering people the promised happiness. The satisfaction we seek is available from a source not made of matter. The happiness we seek is within us at the level of our soul. Bliss, unlimited knowledge, power, fearlessness, happiness, and peace are the riches of the soul. If we can dig in the right place, they will all be ours.

##  Finding Time to Dig

If we knew there were riches buried in our backyard, we would not have any trouble finding time to dig. We would steal every spare moment to take that shovel and search. If we could apply that same level of urgency and commitment to finding our soul, we would find the riches within.

Unfortunately, what do most people do? They spend a few minutes here and there, often with gaps of days, weeks, or months, searching for the spiritual treasures. Expecting success with such little effort is like expecting to earn a medical degree by going to classes or studying only a few minutes every few weeks. Spending only a few minutes occasionally in spiritual pursuit will get us to our goal, but it may take several centuries. Time is ticking away every moment. With each passing motion of the clock's second hand, our life grows shorter and shorter. Every minute is precious. If we wish to uncover the riches of the soul, we need to make the best use of our time.

When we are in pursuit of something we really want, finding time is not difficult. When we are committed to our goal, we find that we stay focused on the task until it is completed. We can hardly tear ourselves away from the work that is going to take us to our cherished goal. It is when we feel we must force ourselves to do something that we have to worry about finding time. Finding time to dig is only a problem when we are not committed to the search. Then we have to discipline ourselves to spend time in whatever task we want to attain. It is a lot easier if we have a strong desire and yearning for the goal.

Similarly, if we have an overwhelming desire to find our soul and unite with the Creator, finding time is not an issue. We will become so engrossed in our inner search that we will lose ourselves in its pursuit.

##  Reaching Our Goal

What are the benefits of discovering our soul? Some people want to find bliss and happiness. Others want the knowledge of what lies beyond this world. For some, conquering fear of death is the motivating factor. For others, it is empowerment that drives them.

Let us not lose precious time. How many of us know someone who was snatched from life unexpectedly? It may have been a child or a teen who passed away; it may have been a loved one. It could have been someone who was in the best of health. When we least expect it, someone we love can die. We do not know when our turn will come. Even if it is not death that takes us, sometimes a sickness can afflict us. Some illnesses are so debilitating we can no longer perform our normal functions in life. It is crucial that we take advantage of the time we have when we are fit, healthy, and functioning. Who knows what will happen?

An anecdote from the life of Kabir Sahib illustrates this point. While visiting Benares, Kabir Sahib always passed by the same man daily, who was always sitting in his garden. One day, Kabir Sahib said to him, "Good Sir, instead of merely sitting in your garden doing nothing, why not sit in meditation and make spiritual progress?"

The man replied, "I have a family. My children are young, and I cannot find enough time for spiritual practices now. But I will practice spirituality when the children grow up."

Years later, after the children had grown up, Kabir Sahib met the same man again. "Now that your children are older, do you find time for meditation?"

This time the man responded, "I am in the process of getting my children married off so they can live independently. As soon as they are all married, I will begin my spiritual practices."

A few years passed, and Kabir Sahib met the man again. He again inquired about the man's spiritual life. "Now that your children are married, do you have time for meditation?"

"My children have grandchildren, and I am watching them grow up, receive an education, and then marry."

Some years passed, and Kabir Sahib returned to find that the man had passed away. Kabir Sahib shook his head and said, "The poor man has spent his whole life thinking he would find time for meditation, and passed away without devoting any time to discover his soul. His mind led him into such a deep attachment to this world that he did not take any time for his own meditations."

We do not want to end up like the man who was always too busy to search for God until it was too late. If we were to take a circle and divide it into three slices, label each slice: "physical goals," "intellectual goals," and "spiritual goals," what would we have in each of these arenas? All three are important. Many people think that when they pursue spiritual goals, they have to give up everything else. That is what Sant Darshan Singh Ji called "negative mysticism." Spirituality can be a path of what he termed "positive mysticism." This means that while pursuing our spiritual goals, we still take care of the other two aspects of our life, our physical existence and our intellectual life. We first need to prioritize. We can live a balanced life and attend to our physical, mental, and spiritual pursuits.

Take, for example, saving money in the bank. What generally happens is that we want to save, but we end up making this our last priority. We pay all our bills first, then we go through our list of needs and wants, thinking that we will save whatever is left over. But sadly, we find that there is never anything left over. Week after week passes and not a penny makes it into our savings account. This is the same thing that happens to our spiritual goals. We tell ourselves that we will meditate after all other duties and chores are done. What happens? Night comes, sleep overtakes us, and another day passes without meditating.

What do financial planners tell us to do if we want to save money? They tell us to make a direct deposit into our savings account as soon as the paycheck comes. They take the savings right off the top as if it were another bill to be paid. In this way, we force ourselves to save. We need to take a similar approach if we are having difficulty finding time to meditate. We need to take our meditation time right off the top. It should be our first priority, because if it is not, it may not even enter into our priority list at all.

 ## Time for Meditation

To find our soul, we need to spend some time daily in meditation. Some scriptures refer to the concept of tithing ten percent. We can tithe one tenth of our day for our soul.

### ∞ Activity ∞

Draw up a time schedule in which time is blocked out for meditation. The time can consist of at least one session or several sessions. The key is to hold that time sacred. We have twenty-one or twenty-two hours to devote to the other areas of our life. Surely we can allow ourselves time each day for spiritual practices. We should not let anything else intervene with our sacred time.

∽

Most people who work to earn their living face time constraints. The forty-hour work week means that five days a week, we need to rise around five or six in the morning, spend an hour to get ready for work, commute to work, and spend eight hours on the job, plus an hour for lunch. Then there is the hour commute home in rush-hour traffic, and an hour spent at home unwinding and having dinner. Thus, thirteen hours of our day are already consumed by work. If we sleep six hours a night, that leaves us with five free hours a day, five days of the week. Where are those five hours? Usually they fall in the evening between the time we return home from work and bedtime. There are several options available to us to find one to two hours a day to meditate. We can spend time in the morning when we wake up. We may have to wake up earlier, but then we assure ourselves that we have already devoted one hour to meditation before the day begins. The other hour needs to come in the evening. Meditation is a good way to unwind after work. One may wish to spend an hour before dinner meditating. Some may prefer meditating an hour before going to sleep. Others enjoy the quiet of the middle of the night or the wee hours of the morning, when everyone else is asleep. For those who work evening or night shifts, the schedule can be reversed. Then, on weekends or days off, we can easily find two to two-and-a-half hours in the day to spend in meditation.

At first, getting used to a schedule may be difficult. Anytime we try to develop a new habit, the mind rebels at first. But, as it is with training in any field, after continued practice, the mind's tendency toward forming habits can be used to our advantage. The mind will become so used to meditating at a certain time, that it will actually feel restless if we skip that time. We need to be patient but firm. Once we establish a schedule, we need to be strong in keeping to it. Ultimately, habit will become second nature, and we will discover that finding time to meditate will become easy and natural.

 ## Taking Time to Save Time

What we may think is taking time, in the long run, can save us time. How? We will experience the benefits of meditation in other areas of our life. Meditation can increase our degree of relaxation so that we require less sleep. The less sleep we need, the more time we have available to us. Meditation also increases our concentration. This means that in tasks that require concentration—for example, our job or our studies—we can work more efficiently and productively. We may find ourselves actually spending less time working or studying because we can complete tasks in a shorter amount of time. Thus, we can actually have more leisure time available to us that were previously spent in study or work.

What can we do with the extra free time? If we use it to meditate, it will be like having bonus cash in the bank. We can increase our progress. We can continue to need less sleep and we can become even more efficient. If we take a look at the lives of those who spend a lot of time in meditation, it is often astounding the amount of work they produce. There are people who do the work of several others at their job with little effort, or they are so prolific in their work, that one wonders how they find time to fit it all in. Sant Darshan Singh used to say, "If you need a job done, who should you go to? Most people think they should go to the one who has nothing to do. Actually, you should find the busiest person. The busiest person can always find time to get a job done." The following account from the life of Sant Kirpal Singh, related in an autobiographical account, gives an example of how one who meditates can find time for many tasks in life and do well in all of them:

> *In the beginning, I asked my Master (Hazur Baba Sawan*
> *Singh) how much time I should devote to the spiritual practices.*
> *Hazur knew fully well that I was a government [civil] servant. I*
> *had to put in eight hours to my service, and I was also a house-*
> *holder with a wife, Krishna Wanti, and my son, Darshan.*
> *Knowing all that, he said, "Devote a minimum of five to six*
> *hours of meditation a day and the more you can do the better."*
> *So what did I do? In the morning I used to sit from three or four*
> *o'clock until nine. I had to. There was no question of whether I*
> *could do it. Then I took my food at twenty minutes after nine*
> *because I had to leave for the office and be there at ten o'clock.*
> *Even the busiest man can find time. Where there is a will there*
> *is a way.*

If we look at the lives of people who achieved greatness in any field, we find that they made their goal a priority. Whether in the field of sports, the arts, entertainment, academics, or business, successful people all put in regular time to accomplish their goals. It is the same in the spiritual field. If we do the work, put in regular time, make meditation a part of our lives, we, too, can achieve success. The cornucopia of spiritual bounties can pour into us, enriching all aspects of our life.

# *Looking Inward and Outward Simultaneously* 15

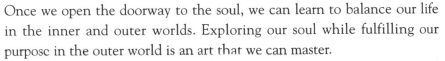

Once we open the doorway to the soul, we can learn to balance our life in the inner and outer worlds. Exploring our soul while fulfilling our purpose in the outer world is an art that we can master.

Spirituality means love in action. It means enjoying our spiritual riches and sharing them with all we meet. We can learn to balance our spiritual practices with our worldly responsibilities, enjoying the fruits within ourselves and sharing our gifts with humanity.

##  Looking Inward

Looking inward means that we are in a state of inner spiritual bliss. We are conscious of our soul's connectedness with God and all life. We are strengthened by the fearlessness that comes with identifying with our soul. We live in the knowledge that we are immortal. Just as a computer monitor is connected to the hard drive and can receive the data from it, we are plugged into and receive a continuous stream from the source of all wisdom, unconditional love, and bliss. We devote specific time to meditation daily, but even when not in meditation, we are in tune with our soul. Throughout the day, as we go about our work, the bliss pours through us, the knowledge is available to us, the fearlessness and strength sustains us, and we are empowered to act on the basis of spiritual values. The stream sustains us from within at all times, enriching every moment of our life.

##  Unlimited Wisdom

By looking inward, we go to the source of wisdom from which all outer knowledge is derived. We may think of wisdom as the state attained by someone who has the highest degree, or someone who has lived through many of life's experience, but these are but a drop of water in the ocean of eternal wisdom. If we took all the books ever written in this world and put them together in one library, they would constitute but a child's primer to the eternal wisdom.

The following story illustrates the difference between worldly knowledge and eternal wisdom. This incident took place when the great scholar Jalaluddin Rumi met his master, the Sufi saint Shamas-i Tabriz. One day, as Rumi sat by the side of a shallow pool studying some rare manuscripts, Shamas-i Tabriz approached him. Seeing that Rumi, the great professor, was lost in study, Tabriz pointed to the manuscript and asked, "What is this?" Looking up at the unkempt visitor, Rumi replied, "It is a knowledge that is beyond the comprehension of the unlearned." Tabriz picked up the book and tossed it into the water. The professor cried out in shock, "Uncouth dervish! What have you done? Through your thoughtless act, the world has lost a treasure house of knowledge." Tabriz reached down to the bottom of the pool and pulled out the manuscript, dry and undamaged. Rumi exclaimed in amazement, "What is this?" Tabriz smiled and said, "It is a knowledge born of ecstasy, that is beyond the comprehension of the learned."

Our mind's comprehension is limited; but the soul's comprehension is infinite. When we look inward, we can reach the state of all-consciousness where we, too, can know everything there is to be known and can be fed from within by the knowledge born of ecstasy.

 ## Immortality

Through meditation we can go beyond the door of death to meet the bliss and beauty that await us beyond. Death no longer holds a sword of fear over us, for in our very lifetime we can see the place where we will go after our body breathes its last. We can finally understand the true meaning of Psalm 23: "Yea, though I walk through the valley of the shadow of death, I will fear no evil for Thou art with me."

Saints who have seen past this world have uttered statements about their views on death. It is not something to fear, they say, but something to embrace. Kabir Sahib has said, "The death of which other people are afraid is a source of happiness for me. It is only with death that I attain everlasting bliss."

St. Teresa of Avila has said of death, "I do not die. I enter into life." For enlightened beings, life as we know it on earth is sleep. Death and entry into the kingdom of God is waking up. St. Paul said, "Oh death, where is thy sting? O grave, where is thy victory?"

We can glimpse the place that is prepared for us beyond the gates of life. Having looked inward to see it, our immortality is no longer a belief but a conviction.

## Fearlessness

By looking inward, we can achieve fearlessness. Behind many fears is fear of loss, pain, and death. Having seen within that there is no death, what is left to fear? What have we to fear when we recognize our soul's connection to God? Those things that are most valuable to us cause us the most pain when they are lost. Sant Kirpal Singh used to say, "If we lose our money, we have lost nothing. If we lose our health, we have lost something. But if we lose our character, we have lost everything." We are measured in the Beyond by our nobility of character and our ethical virtues. Money is of no use there; health is superfluous, for we have no physical body there. Only character counts in the Beyond.

The soul, in its state of oneness with the Lord, fears nothing. It only fears ignorance of that oneness. In reality, sin is merely ignorance of truth. Sin means being unaware of God and the laws of truth and love that govern all the universes. It is a simple formula: virtue is what brings us closer to God, sin or evil takes us away from God. If we walk in the path of righteousness, observing the laws of nonviolence, truthfulness, chastity, humility, and selfless service, and spending time in our spiritual practices of meditation, then we have nothing to fear in this world or in the Beyond.

 ## Unconditional Love

When we look inward, we look into the eyes of unconditional love. God is love, and the soul, being of God's essence, is love. The two merge into one, and the result is eternal bliss. This is the most sublime of unions, the most divine of marriages. Nuptial bliss of this earth is but a small taste of the wondrous bliss from the union with the Lord. Tulsi Sahib has said:

> I have found everlasting fulfillment
> For I am wedded to the Immortal Lord.

This is a union that transcends time and space. It has no beginning; it has no end; but flows ceaselessly. At such a state, we are bathed in this unconditional love within us at all times.

 ## Connectedness

When we are ignorant of our true condition of soul, we may feel disconnected and alone. But when we empower our soul, we are never alone. We are always aware of our connectedness to God and all creation. We realize we have an eternal friend by our side at all times. When we see the same Light that is within our soul in all other souls, we experience connectedness with all forms of life. With such a bond of unity, we realize that all beings are members of our family, and life becomes one joyous reunion with everyone we meet. The joy of family gatherings extends to the whole of humanity. When we journey to any country of the world, we feel at home. No matter who we sit next to at our meals, we feel we are supping with our own family. Love permeates all our dealings, because we are among our universal family and friends.

As Sant Darshan Singh Ji wrote:

> *Others may shun their kith and kin,*
> *But I make even strangers my own.*

By journeying within, we can reach this state and consider all creation our family and all places our home.

 ## Bliss

Unending bliss is ours when we look inward. What is this state like? The great Sufi saint Shamas-i Tabrez has given us a glimpse into this state.

> *Please do not ask me about my inner state of being. My senses, intellect, and soul are intoxicated, and they have achieved a*

*permanent bliss of intoxication. The roots of these trees are drinking the secret wine of love. Have patience, because one day you too will wake up into this state of intoxication. In my mind, there is a festival of intoxication. Feel the effect of the wine of divine love, so that even the walls and door are intoxicated.*

When we are in love with an earthly beloved, the whole world takes on the color of love. We see things as rosy and blissful. Similarly, when in a state of bliss from within, it colors the world as bliss. We then see ecstasy wherever we look.

 ## Looking Outward

While we need to invert to find God, we need not be introverted when dealing with the people around us. Looking outward means that we can also be highly attuned and aware of what is happening in our outer environment. We can place our attention where we choose. Our awareness of the needs of others, our concentration, our sensitivity, and our compassion grow along with our spiritual development. The more we invert, we become aware of the needs of others. One sign that we have grown spiritually is that we are less self-absorbed and selfish and more humanity-absorbed and selfless. The more attuned we are to the soul within us, the greater our love, compassion, and service for our fellow beings.

 ## Looking Outward at Our Workplace

Every aspect of outer life provides an opportunity to be of service to other people. The workplace is rich with such situations.

Many people in management positions become absorbed in their power. Yet true power carries responsibility with it. The higher our position, the more we need to provide help and service to those in lower positions. The following is a beautiful story from the life of Sant Darshan Singh.

> *I learned many important lessons from one of my officers. He would say that the property of power is to protect. Once when a mistake was committed by the staff under him, one of his deputy directors wished to absolve himself of responsibility and said the mistake did not pertain to his section. My officer replied, "This is my directorate and anyone's mistake is my mistake. Even if a peon goes wrong it is my mistake.... Lapses are bound to occur here and there in any work, but throughout my career I always tried to act on the principle I learned from this officer, 'The property of power is to protect.' I considered that any mistake committed by a subordinate was my mistake. I always took the blame myself and gave the explanation myself. Because my superiors trusted me, my explanation would pass off gracefully, where my subordinates would have received some punishment.[1]*

 ## Looking Outward at Planet Earth

As we realize our soul, we also become more aware of planet earth and what is needed to maintain and sustain it. Some people become so sensitive they can feel the pain of lower creatures. They become attuned to the animals and plants and develop compassion and concern for their plight as well.

When Guru Har Rai, the seventh Sikh guru, was a boy, he used to wear a long, flowing robe. One day, he set off by horse to visit his Master, Guru Har Gobind. When he reached his Master's house, he saw him in the garden. Excited to meet him, Har Rai dismounted his horse and rushed through the garden to pay respects to his Master. Before reaching his Master, a sudden breeze blew through the garden, causing Har Rai's robe to flow outward and break several flowers. Har Rai heard the stems cracking and stopped. He saw the damage his robe had caused the plants and it pained him so much that he sat down and began to weep. Another disciple, observing what happened, told Guru Har Gobind what happened. Guru Har Gobind stood up, went over to Har Rai, and asked, "Why are you weeping?" Har Rai explained, "The poor flowers are in pain because I was careless." Guru Har Gobind also had sensitivity for the pain of others, including the plants, and understood Har Rai's despair. He was glad to find that his disciple had that degree of sensitivity. Guru Har Gobind then advised him, "From now on, you may wear these robes, but make sure you hold the skirts close to you when you walk. It is the duty of the servants of God to take care of all forms of life." After that, Har Rai obeyed the advice and always held his robes close to him so he would not injure any plants, insects, or living creatures.

Leonardo da Vinci was a vegetarian. He had a great love of animals, especially birds. He would study birds in flight, and from his observation designed a flying machine, centuries before it became a reality. He could not stand to see the sight of birds captured and caged. Whenever he would see a caged bird, he would purchase it from the owner and then set the bird free.

When we see the outer world through the eyes of our soul, we see the Light of God shining even in plants and animals, and we start to live our lives in such a way as to preserve all living things. As we grow spiritually, we become more receptive to others, including animals and plants. We become more giving and caring when we deal with other people and all forms of life.

 ## Looking Inward and Outward Simultaneously

When we examine the lives of the saints and mystics, we find that they devoted their lives to helping others. They were like the swan that lives in water but flies with dry wings. While all the time they are in tune with the Creator, they still live amongst others, participating fully in life.

The Christian mystic, John Ruysbroeck, has said that "the truly inward man should flow out to all in common." St. Catherine of Genoa, born in the fifteenth century, had a mystic experience in which she was transported to a state of pure and purifying love for God. Her mystical revelation was followed by a life of selfless service to others. She began working to help the sick and the poor. At the age of thirty, she founded the first hospital in the city of Genoa. For the next twenty-two years, she lived in a state of continued consciousness with the divine presence of the Lord filling her with joy, love, and bliss. Yet while she experienced perpetual ecstasy, she continued managing the hospital. She was punctual and efficient in her duties at the hospital and never let her spiritual absorption keep her from fulfilling her worldly responsibilities. When a plague swept through Genoa, she formed a group to nurse the victims. In a conversation with God, she once said, "You have ordered me to love my neighbor, yet I cannot love anything but You." God told her, "One who loves me, loves all that I love." Thus, she showed her love for God through love for her fellow beings and all forms of life, including plants and animals. It was said of her, "If an animal were killed or a tree were cut down, she could hardly bear to see them lose the life that God had given them."

In the four stages of ardent love, St. Richard of Victor describes the stages of betrothal, marriage, wedlock, and the fruitfulness of the soul. In the betrothal stage, the soul thirsts for God. It has a ruling passion to experience higher reality. The soul is touched by the spirit of God and is bathed in sweetness. This is the stage of the soul's awakening. In the second stage, the soul is burning with desire for God and is taken as the bride of the Lord. The soul ascends, sees the sun of righteousness, and takes the marriage vows to God. In the third stage, the soul has union with the Lord. The soul is in communion with God, is fully concentrated on God, and caught up in the divine Light. In the fourth stage of ardent love, we find the crux of the life of a true mystic: giving of one's spiritual wealth to humanity. The union of the soul with the Lord is not a childless union. The soul takes on the responsibilities, duties, and pains of parenthood to bring forth children. The children here are represented by good and noble works in the world that serve humanity. The empowered souls become centers of spiritual energy and are conscious co-workers of the divine plan. They live out their lives spreading spiritual love to all they meet, inspiring and uplifting others by their example.

We, too, can attain this state. By spending time daily in meditation, we can discover the power of our soul, enriching our lives with wisdom, immortality, love, fearlessness, connectedness, and bliss.

# *Endnotes*

## Chapter 4: Unconditional Love

1 *Mysticism*. Underhill, Evelyn. (New York: E. P. Dutton, 1911), p. 286

2 Ibid., p. 426

## Chapter 7: Bliss

1 *Streams of Nectar: Lives, Poetry, and Teachings of Saints and Mystics*. Singh. Darshan. (Naperville, Illinois: SK Publications, 1993), p. 185

2 *Mysticism*. Underhill, Evelyn. (New York: E. P. Dutton, 1911), p. 369–370

3 *The Spiritual Path: Anthology of the Writings of Kirpal Singh*. (Naperville, Illinois: SK Publications, 1994), p. 65

4 Ibid., 65

5 Ibid., p. 205

6 *The Varieties of Religious Experience.* James, William. (New York: Mentor Books, 1958), p. 314–315

7 *Streams of Nectar: Lives, Poetry, and Teachings of Saints and Mystics.* Singh, Darshan. (Naperville, Illinois: SK Publications, 1993), p. 151

8 Ibid., p. 152

9 *The Varieties of Religious Experience.* James, William. (New York: Mentor Books, 1958), p. 318

## Chapter 11: Meditation: Doorwary to the Soul

1 *The Crown of Life.* Singh, Kirpal (Bowling Green, Virginia: SK Publications, 1985), p. 143

2 *The Jap Ji.* Singh, Kirpal (Bowling Green, Virginia: SK Publications, 1987), p. 27

3 Ibid., p. 27

## Chapter 15: Looking Inward and Outward Simulataneously

1 *Love Has Only a Beginning: Autobiography of Darshan Singh.* Singh, Darshan. (Naperville, Illinois: SK Publications, 1996), pp. 93–94

# *About the Author*

Sant Rajinder Singh is an internationally-recognized expert teacher of meditation and head of Science of Spirituality, a non-profit, non-denominational organization that provides a forum for people to learn meditation, experience personal transformation, and bring about inner and outer peace and human unity.

He has presented his powerful, yet simple technique to millions of people throughout the world through seminars, meditation retreats, television and radio shows, magazines, and books. His method of achieving inner and outer peace through meditation has been recognized by civic, religious, and spiritual leaders. He convened the 16th International Human Unity Conference in Delhi, India; was president of the 7th World Religions Conference; was a major presenter at the Parliament of the World Religions held in Chicago in 1993 and the World Conference on Religion and Peace held in Rome and Riva del Garde, Italy, in 1994; and hosts annual international conferences on Human Integration and Global Mysticism. At the 50th Anniversary of the United Nations celebration held at the Cathedral of St. John the Divine, Rajinder Singh opened the program by putting thousands of people into meditation.

He has received numerous awards, tributes and honorary welcomes from civic and religious heads around the world.

He has written several books, including *Inner and Outer Peace through Meditation* (Element Books), *Visions of Spiritual Unity and Peace, Ecology of the Soul, Education for a Peaceful World,* and in Hindi, *Spirituality in Modern Times* and *True Happiness,* audiotapes, and video-tapes, as well as hundreds of articles which have been published in magazines, newspapers, and journals throughout the world. His publications have been translated into fifty languages. He has been broadcast on many television and radio programs throughout the world.

Rajinder Singh holds meditation seminars and gives public lectures throughout Europe, North America, South America, Africa, Asia, and Australia. He can be contacted at Kirpal Ashram, Kirpal Marg, Vijay Nagar, Delhi, India 110009; Tele: 91-11-7222244 or 7223333; or FAX: 91-11-7214040; or at Science of Spirituality Center, 4 S. 175 Naperville Rd., Naperville, IL 60563; Tele: (630) 955-1200; or FAX: (630) 955-1205.